Sacred
DECISIONS
Consensus in Faith Communities

Marcia J. Patton | Nora J. Percival

Foreword by Eric H. F. Law

JUDSON PRESS
PUBLISHERS SINCE 1824
VALLEY FORGE, PA

Sacred Decisions: Consensus in Faith Communities
© 2021 by Judson Press, Valley Forge, PA 19482-0851
All rights reserved.

No part of this publication may be reproduced, stored in a retrieval system, or transmitted in any form or by any means, electronic, mechanical, photocopying, recording, or otherwise, without the prior permission of the copyright owner, except for brief quotations included in a review of the book.

Judson Press has made every effort to trace the ownership of all quotes. In the event of a question arising from the use of a quote, we regret any error made and will be pleased to make the necessary correction in future printings and editions of this book.

Bible quotations in this volume are from the New Revised Standard Version of the Bible, copyright © 1989 by the Division of Christian Education of the National Council of the Churches of Christ in the United States of America. Used by permission. All rights reserved.

Interior design by Beth Oberholtzer.
Cover design by Danny Ellison.

Library of Congress Cataloging-in-Publication data

Names: Patton, Marcia, author. | Percival, Nora J, author.
Title: Sacred decisions : consensus in faith communities / Marcia J. Patton and Nora J. Percival.
Description: Valley Forge, PA : Judson Press, 2021.
Identifiers: LCCN 2021017883 (print) | LCCN 2021017884 (ebook) | ISBN 9780817018290 (paperback) | ISBN 9780817082321 (epub)
Subjects: LCSH: Church group work. | Group decision making. | Decision making--Religious aspects--Christianity. | Christian leadership.
Classification: LCC BV652.2 .P38 2021 (print) | LCC BV652.2 (ebook) | DDC 253/.7--dc23
LC record available at https://lccn.loc.gov/2021017883
LC ebook record available at https://lccn.loc.gov/2021017884

Printed in the U.S.A.

First printing, 2021.

■ ■ ■

*To the people of Evergreen Association
of American Baptist Churches,
for their courage to listen to each other and God,
and embrace a new way to do God's work in the world.*

Contents

Foreword	vii
Acknowledgments	xiii
Introduction	xv
CHAPTER ONE: Why Use Consensus?	2
CHAPTER TWO: What Is Consensus?	14
CHAPTER THREE: Step by Step	21
CHAPTER FOUR: The Facilitator	42
CHAPTER FIVE: Consensus Takes Time	58
CHAPTER SIX: Dos & Don'ts	66
CHAPTER SEVEN: Virtual Meetings	82
Epilogue	91
APPENDIX 1: Sample Agenda	93
APPENDIX 2: Sample Communication Tools	95
APPENDIX 3: Sample Group Norms	97
APPENDIX 4: Levels of Consensus	99
APPENDIX 5: Suggested Issues to Use for Practice	100

Foreword

I have known Marcia Patton since the early formation days of the Evergreen Association of American Baptist Churches, for which she was the executive minister. I admired her uncompromising dedication to ensuring that people of diverse racial and cultural backgrounds were included in every level of the organization. After she retired from being the executive minister of Evergreen, she accepted my invitation to be the president of the Kaleidoscope Institute for sustainable and diverse communities. Marcia is one of those pastors who is always learning from the experiences from which she reaps her gifts for ministries. Through teaching and writing, she propagates these learnings so that more people can be empowered by these gifts.

Of course, no one can do this in isolation. Marcia's encounter with Nora Percival was providential, and their partnership was sewn together by their shared commitment to equality and community. Practicing consensus in their partnership, Marcia and Nora have been describing and teaching the foundational process of consensus decision-making, resulting in this book: *Sacred Decisions: Consensus in Faith Communities*. As they say in the Introduction: "Equality means that every person's voice is equally important, and community means that the people in the room are more important than the decision under discussion" (p. xvi).

While this book was being put together, I invited Marcia and Nora to teach a segment of a Kaleidoscope Institute Gracious

Leadership training program for a group of pastors from diverse racial and cultural backgrounds. In the short time they were given, they shared with clarity and ease the sacred decision process outlined in this book. The inter-supportive connections between the consensus process and the Gracious Leadership skills were like pieces of cloth carefully laid out and sewn together to make a patchwork quilt that provides comfort and safety for a community learning to make sacred decisions. (I use this analogy because Marcia is a fantastic visionary quilter.) When this process is learned and practiced, phrases that capture the essence of consensus decision-making—will remain a part of the community's lexicon even after the decision has been made. These include:

> "How we work together is as important as what we do."
>
> "The people in the room are more important than the decision in question."
>
> "We are ready to live with the decision we are making."
>
> "We agree not to work or speak against the decision once it is made."

As more and more members of the organization live into this culture of consensus, the whole community will be transformed. Others will notice this graciousness too, and the organization will become a light of truth and grace in a world of polarization and destructive decision-making.

Every decision is an opportunity for a community to move toward its goals and mission in unity and with grace. Every decision also has the danger of leading to harmful power plays and legal issues in the future. As leaders, we need to intentionally choose processes and methods that enable our community to stay in unity after the decision is made. This needs to be intentional because, without a clearly defined consensus process, many groups will tend to allow political and legal instincts to drive the decision-making process.

For instance, at a church council meeting, an enthusiastic church member asked, "Should we open our parking lot to let the community college students park during the week?" Having done some research on the need for parking spaces for the growing number of students at the community college just a block away, this church member thought this would be a great way to welcome young people, a population that the church had tried unsuccessfully to reach in the last twenty years. While she expected a discussion—and hopefully a positive decision—at this meeting, an influential member said, "If we let them park in our lot and they get into trouble like an accident, or get caught doing drugs, we are liable to be sued." Another influential member agreed, and that was the end of the discussion. The decision was made, resulting in the majority of the council members feeling shut out and resentful.

Imagine if this same church council had invited its members to read and practice the processes in this book. How could they have approached this parking lot opportunity using consensus decision-making? I imagine the process would have included more listening, exploration, and the consideration of creative solutions such as inviting students to sign a covenant if they are to park there. Even if, in the end, the decision was "no," the council members would still be able to work together congenially.

Sometimes there is a commitment to using consensus, but the process is not clearly defined, so the legal and political drives might take over. As in the case of a church in a diverse neighborhood that was in pastoral transition and created a search committee to present a short list of candidates for the senior pastor position. The committee decided to make all decisions by consensus, but they did not have this book to guide them, and consensus was never clearly defined. As a result, a few members thought it meant everyone had to agree for a potential candidate to make the list. One politically/legally inclined person rejected any candidates he did not like, and no one would contradict him as he reminded the group that, legally, everyone had to agree. The final list of candidates was composed only of white men in their forties—which this one person thought the profile of a senior pastor should be. When the diverse church congregation found out about this list of candidates, there were disappointed, angry, and some even threatened to leave.

What if the same search committee members had read this book? With a clearly defined process, the resulting decisions might have been very different. More importantly, working through the consensus process might have enabled the church community to live with the search committee's decisions.

Throughout this book, there are many such real-life examples and personal witnesses from leaders who have used the consensus decision-making process successfully. *Sacred Decisions* provides a template for creating the sacred ground that avoids the dangerous domination of the legal and political, while helping the community focus and spend time discerning the people's needs and interests. This does not mean that we ignore the legal and political implications of decision-making. Rather, it is a matter of transforming potentially harmful legal and political patterns through a consensus process. A sacred decision directs the community to listen to the truth and experiences of the people first. Then, based on what they've heard, a decision can be made legally, in the sense of it being the right thing to do, and politically, in terms of who will be empowered to implement the decision and be truly supported by the community. When this is done well, legally and politically inclined persons should be able to live with and support the decision, even though they might not have gotten what they wanted in the process.

This book is for the leaders of churches and organizations who are tired of endless debates, arguments that shut down creativity, the powerful few controlling every decision and sabotaging others' actions, some voices being neither valued nor heard, and angry communications/threats after a decision is made. Even if you are a leader who already uses consensus decision-making, this book will help you clarify and improve your methods. Marcia and Nora move our understanding of consensus from theoretical to practical, from defining to implementing, from "why" to "how," from dogmatic to theological, and from narrowness to grace.

Share *Sacred Decisions* with others in your church or organization. Use this book to train all the leaders who have the responsibility of assisting groups in decision-making. Plan a meeting using the step-by-step process laid out in this book. I truly believe that when this process is practiced throughout your church or organization, over time it will be recognized by the surrounding community as a sacred ground where people are honored, truth is discerned together, and difficult decision-making is worked through to arrive at resolutions that are holistic, creative, and regenerative.

The Rev. Dr. Eric H. F. Law, DD
Founder and Innovator
Kaleidoscope Institute
for diverse and sustainable communities

Acknowledgments

In addition to working together on this book, we would like to thank many others who have contributed to it.

We are grateful to the people who shared their experiences with consensus in this book: Rev. Douglas Avilesbernal, Executive Minister of Evergreen Association of American Baptist Churches, for their annual meeting story; Rev. Sean Brown, pastor of Wedgwood Community Church, for their story of learning to use consensus; Dr. Dorsey Green, former clerk of Friends Committee for National Legislation and University Friends Meeting, for the story about approving same-sex marriage; and Jill Wynns, a twenty-four-year veteran of the San Francisco Board of Education and past president of the California School Boards Association (and Nora's sister), for the story about consensus and public policy development.

We are also grateful to those who contributed their wisdom: Jeff Johnson for the succinct explanation of the *good order of Friends*, Rev. Dr. Eric Law for his work in developing Mutual Invitation and RESPECT guidelines, and Ben Richmond for the reference to Jesus in Gethsemane giving up his human will to God's will.

When we first assembled the manuscript, we approached trusted leaders and friends to read it and give feedback. Their comments and suggestions were helpful beyond words, and we give our great gratitude to Leslie Beckett, Asia Bennett, Rev. Dr. Eric Law, Carolyn Stevens, and Rev. Dr. Jeff Woods.

Last but not least, our heartfelt thanks go to Judson Press for believing in our work and helping us share it with you.

Introduction

Our story begins at a Church Council of Greater Seattle (CCGS) event. Planners had asked Marcia to offer a workshop on consensus based on her work with the Evergreen Association of American Baptist Churches. As a board member of CCGS and a Quaker, Nora attended Marcia's workshop to see how non-Quakers used consensus.

Marcia asked the participants of the workshop to introduce themselves and their faith communities. When Nora introduced herself as a Quaker, Marcia was flabbergasted. What did she have to offer to someone belonging to a faith that has used consensus for more than 360 years? But gracious as ever, she invited Nora to add her Quaker perspective to the workshop. Nora had joined the session mostly out of curiosity, but she was happy to step up and contribute her experience and perspective.

At the end of the session, Nora approached Marcia. She was excited by the idea of consensus working well in any faith community, not just her own, and wanted to do more workshops with Marcia. Marcia was also interested in this, and they set a date to meet for lunch and discuss future possibilities. So began our journey together to share our passion for using consensus in faith communities and to show people how much of a positive difference it can make in the life of a community.

Marcia came to know consensus while working on the establishment of the Evergreen Association of American Baptist Churches. Before Evergreen was created, its member churches had been part of American Baptist Churches of the Northwest

NW). After two contentious biennial meetings that used majority rule, *Robert's Rules of Order*, and a trained parliamentarian, the churches that eventually became Evergreen left ABC-NW to form a new association.

When the churches of Evergreen started writing the bylaws for the new organization, they knew that majority rule was not going to serve their needs. In addition to their recent painful experiences with ABC-NW, Evergreen had created a unique structure based on ethnic caucuses, and they knew that voting would undermine the goals of this structure. (See the end of Chapter 2 for a more complete story of the creation of Evergreen's consensus process.) They eventually decided to make decisions by consensus and began by adopting the bylaws by consensus. Almost two decades later, Evergreen continues to operate based on consensus and to grow in size and strength.

Quakers have been using a form of consensus since 1655. Michael Sheeran has described the process well: "Central to the Quaker understanding of unity-based decision-making is ... the ... idea that there is 'that of God in everyone.' When a group of believers comes together to deliberate about the best way to serve God here and now, each expects to find in others some manifestation of 'that of God's' and looks for the mark of the Spirit of Christ—Truth with a capital 'T'—in everyone else's remarks. In short, since the same Spirit speaks in each heart, the members expect to end their meetings united."[1]

When Nora first became a Quaker as a young adult, she learned the Quaker testimonies of simplicity, peace, integrity, community, and equality (SPICE) and used them as guidelines for living a God-centered life. As she became more familiar with the Quaker process for making decisions, she began to appreciate how deeply rooted it is in the testimonies of equality and community. Equality means that every person's voice is equally important, and community means that the people in the room are more important than the decision under discussion. As she has used Quaker process in groups of all sizes facing both great and small issues, she has come to see how profoundly consensus helps faith groups stay focused on God's will for them.

We do our best to practice consensus in all aspects of our lives. In fact, we wrote this book using consensus. Because of how important this kind of decision-making is to both of us, we invite you to try using it too, to see what a difference it can make in your faith community.

We are well aware as we write this that we are speaking only for ourselves. Both of our faith traditions are grounded in "soul freedom," meaning not only do we each face our Creator without intervention by another, but everyone else does too. Therefore, we do not speak for all Quakers or all American Baptists. We write about our traditions in this book from our personal perspectives, and we do not presume to say that all Quakers or all American Baptists necessarily agree with us.

We have included stories at the end of each chapter to give you real-world examples of how consensus works (and how it doesn't work when it is not done well). Some of them come from our personal experiences. We have also asked trusted colleagues to share their stories, to give you a wider variety of perspectives on the benefits and challenges of using consensus.

■ ■ ■

We all make many decisions every day. When we are part of a group, faith-based or secular, we make and live with our decisions as a group. Most organizations use one method for making most or all decisions. Some choose to have one person in charge make decisions, that is, autocratically; others choose to let a small group of chosen leaders make decisions, that is, oligarchically. Most American faith communities make decisions by voting, that is, by majority rule.

Majority rule is familiar to millions of people. The ancient Greeks invented it, the Romans refined it, and the United States has used it at all levels of government for more than 230 years. Most of us learned how to use it as children in school. However, majority rule has some significant pitfalls. It is intrinsically adversarial; the majority opinion is heard and validated, but the minority is silenced. The community is, by definition, divided into winners and losers. The losers often want to undermine the decision they didn't choose. If they can't, they often leave the community, which impoverishes it. Even when the losers stay, they often carry bitterness toward the decision, and by extension, toward the community.

There is an alternative: consensus-based decision-making. It is a different way to think about making decisions. No action is taken until all stakeholders can live with implementing the decision. Perhaps not everyone loves the decision, but all are able to accept it as the will of the group as a whole. If you think that cannot work, think about what happened in the wake of your community's last major decision. Did everyone go forward from the decision point committed to implementing it and feeling accepting of everyone else in the group? Wouldn't it be worth trying something new to have that outcome?

If you think that, because you're not a Quaker or a rogue Baptist, this just won't work for you, be reassured that many organizations use one version or another of consensus quite successfully. The North Atlantic Treaty Organization and the European Council of the European Union both make decisions by consensus (and they have made some world-defining decisions). Virtually all Quaker organizations, such as the American Friends Service Committee, have always made decisions this way. In many traditional cultures, local communities make decisions by consensus, and several contemporary regional governments (e.g., two Canadian provinces and the island of Guernsey) use a form of it.

Americans tend to think of voting and majority rule as sacrosanct because federal and state governments in the US use them. They have a hard time even considering alternatives. This is ironic considering that the US Constitution was created through a process (promoted by Benjamin Franklin) noted for its openness to new ideas, rejection of one-sided advocacy, and regard for creative compromise.[2] These are all foundational themes of consensus-building.

Many churches act as though *Robert's Rules of Order*,[3] the most widely used manual for conducting meetings by majority rule, is as sacred as the Bible. Yet there is no theological or historical requirement to do this and letting go of the need to use majority rule can give your community an increased sense of unity.

However, it takes practice to unlearn generations of majority-rule thinking, especially to let go of the expectation that there will be winners and losers. It is best to practice consensus decision-making and get comfortable with how it works before you need to use the process for a critical decision. Try it out first with a small group, such as an executive committee or work group, before introducing it to a larger group. Then try using it with the larger group for decisions that are not controversial and don't have a major impact on the community. Then when a big decision comes up, you know how to begin the process of addressing it as a group, and you have the confidence that the process will strengthen rather than damage the community.

Although any group can use the processes we describe in this book, we readily admit that we are Christians and come from a faith-based perspective. As a Quaker and an American Baptist, we each think a bit differently about consensus, but we believe that this makes our collaborative work less denominationally specific and therefore more relevant to a wider audience. The ideas and suggestions we present here are specifically intended to be used in faith communities of all kinds, but many of them can also work in secular situations.

Faith-based consensus is really a communal seeking of God's will. Quakers call this "the sense of the meeting." At root, it is not actually consensus, but rather looking for a decision from the absolute ruler of the community, God. It is akin to autocracy, with the difference that it takes everyone in the community to discern what the ruler, God, wants the community to do. The process we describe in this book is a set of techniques for peeling away the assumptions, biases, and prejudices that we, as humans, bring to our decision-making, so we can clearly hear what God is telling us to do.

We offer this book to congregational leaders and others who want to try using consensus and need help getting started. We intend it to be a "how-to" resource for those who are interested in changing how they make group decisions, but do not know where to begin. The stories at the end of the chapters are offered to illustrate how the principles of consensus are applied in real situations. We look forward to hearing how you use the ideas we present here and how consensus decision-making changes your community.

Please note that, though we may speak in generalities in this book, we are speaking from our own experiences using faith-based consensus to make decisions in our Quaker and American Baptist organizations. We know it works because we use it in our faith communities. We are confident that it can work in your community too.

Notes:

1. Michael J. Sheeran, S.J., *Beyond Majority Rule: voteless decisions in the Religious Society of Friends* (Denver: Regis College, 1983), 3–4.

2. See Walter Isaacson, *Benjamin Franklin, An American Life* (New York: Simon & Shuster, 2003); Chapter Sixteen: Sage, Subchapter: The Constitutional Convention of 1787, for more about Benjamin Franklin's moderating influence on the constitutional convention.

3. *Robert's Rules of Order* is the most widely used manual of parliamentary procedure in the United States. Written by Henry Martyn Robert and first published in 1876, it describes a set of precepts and procedures for conducting meetings where decisions are made by majority rule. Robert's primary purpose in writing the book was to enable groups to make as many decisions as possible that the majority of group members supported in the minimum amount of time. He further intended that his rules would make this possible regardless of the range and/or intensity of opinions in the group at the beginning of the meeting.

Consensus

We reach consensus when all of us are ready to live with the decision we are making. We do not all have to endorse it wholeheartedly, but we must all be ready to agree not to work or speak against the decision once it is made. Until we come to that point, our tasks are to share our ideas respectfully, listen to each other with open hearts, and find together what God wants us to do.

CHAPTER ONE
Why Use Consensus?

When we talk to people about consensus, the first question is often, "Why? Why bother to change the way we do our work, especially to a more complex and subtle process? Why not just keep making decisions as we always have? Majority rule has gotten us this far."

It is understandable that your group may want to stay with majority rule, since most of us have used it at school and work for most of our lives. Remarkably, even though faith communities are fundamentally different from secular ones, most of us have always also used majority rule at church. In all group settings, people tend to resist change and want life to be familiar, so they hold on to majority rule because they know how to do it. In the minds of many people, voting works fine, and they think, "Why fix it if it isn't broken?" However, although voting may work some of the time, the results can be disastrously far-reaching when it does not work. When that happens, it is too late to avoid calamity by considering a different model for making group decisions.

With nothing to compare it to, many people think that voting is the only way for a group to make decisions. It is not. Consensus is a different approach to group problem-solving. It often works better than majority rule, especially when majority rule is not serving the needs of your community.

Our world is complicated. Simple questions seem to have complex answers, and for many questions, there is never just one answer. This is as true in faith communities as it is in secular organizations. What seems simple to one person seems more complex to the next person. What is self-evident to one is not so obvious to others. In this difficult time, when so many faith communities seek peace and therefore need to promote justice, it is often unclear what constitutes justice or peace. Just two people discussing peace and justice can struggle to see these the same way; when you add more and especially more diverse voices, the complexity increases.

Given the wide range of human attitudes toward just about everything, some people think consensus unnecessarily complicates the decision-making process further, rather than helping it. But the very thing we need for justice is to hear and understand all sides. Majority rule often silences the voices that need to be considered most in a decision, while consensus creates space for those voices to be heard.

If your group feels fractured or stressed, with underlying tensions and personality conflicts coloring its work, your decision-making model is probably not serving you well. Perhaps your faith community is striving, as so many are now, to discern how to make a difference for those who have been hurt, marginalized, or misunderstood. If so, consensus is an inherently just way to make decisions, making it easier for everyone to be heard and appreciated. Instead of your whole group having to go along with what the majority believes, you can search together to discover what God is calling you to do.

When you use consensus, it is easier to make decisions that everyone can support. In addition, the process itself affects community interaction in many positive ways.

- It promotes inclusivity.
- It is more egalitarian and less patriarchal.
- It encourages a collaborative spirit.
- It fosters the emergence of unanticipated, better solutions.

- It offers an alternative to avoiding issues for fear of stirring up trouble.
- It demonstrates the belief that everyone's voice is important.
- It shows that the people in the room are more important than the decision in question.
- It embodies the belief that how we work together is as important as what we do.
- It clearly invites God into the process.

It promotes inclusivity, which makes the community more welcoming and more robust. We have deliberately chosen to use the term *inclusivity* in this book. Any group can be diverse just by including people with different demographics. To be truly inclusive, your group must intentionally ensure that everyone's voice is heard, and further, that everyone's ideas, thoughts, experiences, and gifts have an influence on the outcome. This gives everyone in the group a sense of ownership in the process, which is how you achieve authentic inclusion.

When every person feels like their point of view is heard, they feel included. As a result, the discussions (and often the results) are more dynamic and holistic. Majority rule automatically excludes the minority. The voting process inherently sets up haves and have-nots; it counts the losers as much as the winners. Even when you use secret ballots, people know when their choice loses and their point of view is disregarded. Using majority rule, you can lose from the start, but by using consensus, you can create a welcoming place for everyone. If your goal is peace, being inclusive is a necessity. If you seek to have a more inclusive community, consensus can help you achieve it, because to reach authentic consensus, everyone must hear everyone else.

Evergreen's decision to use consensus for making group decisions has been key to making their ethnic caucus structure work. Before choosing a decision-making method, they had already embraced the inclusive ideas of basing their structure on ethnic causes, rotating officers by caucus, and defining a quorum as at least one person from each caucus. Then they decided to use consensus to make decisions and to use the caucuses as the vehicle for ensuring that every voice is heard. As a result of these decisions, every caucus has an equal voice in making decisions even though they are not of equal size. The respect that this engenders among the caucuses is amazing. The Euro caucus, far larger than the other caucuses, can be open to true partnership with the other caucuses, and the other caucuses, with smaller memberships, can use their voices with clarity.

It is more egalitarian and less patriarchal. When done well, consensus helps every person have an equal voice. As a result, it is harder for one individual or faction to have a disproportionate influence on the outcome of a discussion. Everyone has an equal opportunity to contribute, and no one group, or individual is heard more than the others. As with any group process, consensus can be derailed by the "tyranny of the loud," with naturally dominating personalities bullying others into agreeing before they have formulated their own opinions. However, this rarely happens when consensus is done well, because the structure of the process encourages people to be heard. All participants have equal standing and equal opportunity for input.

It encourages a collaborative spirit. When done well, consensus requires that everyone listen carefully to everyone else. Individuals or cliques with strong preconceived opinions or who want to dominate the group have a chance to be heard, but shy people with good ideas have the same chance. When your group commits to really taking the time to hear everyone's concerns about an issue, everyone can feel part of the decision, satisfied that their considerations are included. This is the embodiment of true collaboration; when done conscientiously, it becomes almost impossible for one person or faction to dominate the rest of the group. Participants are empowered to resist the urge to be swayed by the loudest voice or strongest opinion, and instead, to look within themselves for their own understanding, to share it, and to listen with open hearts to everyone else's sharing.

It fosters the emergence of unanticipated, better solutions. When everyone in a meeting takes the time and has the benevolence to hear everyone else, a new understanding of the issue by the group as a whole often emerges. We call this the "miracle of consensus," and it is a delightful surprise every time it happens. New ideas emerge and render the solutions initially proposed (and sometimes even the original questions) irrelevant. This often leads to better decisions than anyone imagined possible before the discussion. It doesn't happen all the time, but when it does, it demonstrates how powerfully consensus can help your group make good decisions. With parliamentary procedure, an issue has to be introduced with a proposed solution, which implies that those who raise the question already know the answer. With consensus, you can raise an issue for discussion without a pre-conceived solution and let the best outcome emerge from the discussion.

It offers an alternative to avoiding issues for fear of stirring up trouble. When you use consensus, it is easier to bring up difficult or complex issues because you do not have to come to a decision right away. Once your group is familiar with the process, individuals develop confidence that bringing up an issue as soon as it arises is good, as it allows time for the salient questions to work in people's minds and hearts. Your group members learn to tackle complex issues together with hope, because they trust that eventual resolutions will be acceptable to everyone. In contrast, majority rule usually rushes to a decision based on the judgment of those with the most compelling initial argument, because it convinces the most people initially. But initial arguments often overlook the full ramifications of a decision. Because consensus requires time, it is more likely to bring everyone to an understanding of the whole picture.

It demonstrates the belief that everyone's voice is important. With every meeting and every decision, your group's members increase their trust that their ideas will not be ignored. In seeking justice, this is a necessity. People do not feel like their voices are heard unless they actually can give their opinions and have them received with respect. Authentic justice requires that every voice is heard. With majority rule, most people do not have their voices heard. We know from experience that those who vote on the losing side of a decision often feel completely unheard. You might think that everyone who votes with the majority feels heard, but many of them will have agreed only partially with the majority decision. All those unheard "minor" concerns will undermine the strength of the community as the decision is implemented. The community is strongest when everyone has a voice that is respected.

It shows that the people in the room are more important than the decision in question. *Robert's Rules of Order* and majority rule keep things humming along in a prescribed way, but they often leave individuals and factions within your group marginalized. Because the majority does not need to hear or value the minority to make a decision, those in the minority often feel unheard and undervalued. Too often, we consider the decision, whatever it is, to be more important than the people it might affect. This order of priorities is backward, especially in a faith community. Also, when you take the time to include a thorough discussion of all the issues, it takes a bit more time, but you often come to a better decision.

It embodies the belief that how we work together is as important as what we do. As the Quakers say, "Process is our most important product." Honoring the importance of how you work together may already be a priority of your faith community. However, when you use majority rule to make group decisions, you tell your community that the minority opinion is not as worthy as the majority view. In contrast, when you use consensus, you demonstrate your belief in the importance of valuing every member's contribution.

It is valuable in general to think more deeply about how your group makes decisions and not just accept your habitual method without examining it. When you take the time to consider how you work together as a community, you show that you value the group process itself, not just the decisions that come out of it. This is true regardless of the actual process you use, and sometimes just the act of examining your current decision-making rules can improve them.

It clearly invites God into the process, which is most important for a faith community. Although this is not said often enough, even in this book, when human beings come to authentic agreement, it is evidence of God at work. For many people, majority rule is legitimized by the assumption that God is with the majority, but actually, most denominations and Christianity itself started as small groups with minority views. Using consensus allows your community to shed the expectation that God will take sides and replace it with corporately seeking the mind of Christ. When you accept that God knows what the best decision is and that your job is to discern God's will, you are following the example of Jesus when he prayed in Gethsemane. At first, he pleaded to be spared the ordeal he knew was coming, but in the end, he surrendered to God's will. Mark recorded it thus: "And going a little farther, he threw himself on the ground and prayed that, if it were possible, the hour might pass from him. He said, 'Abba Father, for you all things are possible; remove this cup from me; yet, not what I want, but what you want'" (Mark 14:35-36).

It is easy to think that you know what God wants you to do before you begin to discuss an issue, but only when you really listen to each other can you truly come to know God's will for your whole community. Quakers aspire to enter every meeting for business ready to have their minds changed. This is not easy; it takes time, persistence, and humility. Ironically, it is often hardest and most necessary when we start out certain that God is on our side. We can only truly know what God wants for us by listening to everyone's sense of God's will, for as long as it takes to hear everyone. This process of exploring more deeply together to find what God might be saying often leads to very different answers than anyone considered at the beginning of the process, and sometimes even different questions. When compared to the power of a faith community seeking God's will, the arguments against consensus lose their force.

■ ■ ■

When you make decisions using majority rule, there are virtually always winners and losers. Every once in a great while, there is a unanimous vote, but most of the time, some part of your group loses out. These people often leave the meeting feeling dismissed. If they did not support the decision that was made, they might also want to see it fail, to validate their inner attitude of "I knew it was a bad idea." As a result, your group can become fractured, with some members resentful of being pushed aside and ready to undermine the implementation of the decision.

Also, when you use voting to make decisions, it is easy for stronger personalities to coerce others to follow their lead. Especially when you vote by a show of hands, many people let the most charismatic people in the room decide how they should vote. Coercion can happen in a consensus process too, but not as easily, and there are many ways to limit it.

When a community moves from voting to consensus, there is a profound shift in group dynamics. Consensus invites everyone to participate, which creates a more welcoming community. People feel heard and therefore included, leading them to feel empowered to contribute, even those who, in other circumstances, might consider their contributions unworthy.

Consensus is intrinsically egalitarian as well as just. Creating a space to hear every voice regardless of age, gender, or social standing helps your group transcend the patriarchal social norms that prevail in our society. It also helps disempower individuals and cliques that want to dominate the group. And it can help your group stop avoiding issues for fear of stirring up trouble you don't know how to resolve.

Spiritually, it allows your community to embody the beliefs that everyone's voice is important and that the people in the room are more important than the decision in question. It also gives your community the experience of valuing how you work together as much as you value what you do. Most important for faith communities, it clearly invites God into your business process and deeper into the life of your community.

When your group does the work to learn how to use consensus and begins to receive the gifts it offers, the group becomes stronger and more responsive to members' needs. It also demonstrates its commitment to God, as in Micah 6:8. Surely there is no more crucial time than this for your community and world to become more resilient and vigorous by committing to live your faith.

Wedgwood Community Church's Experience With Consensus

BY REV. SEAN BROWN

Rev. Sean Brown is the pastor of Wedgwood Community Church, a 100-year-old, small, mostly Euro-American congregation in a residential neighborhood in Seattle. Wedgwood is one of the first Evergreen churches to choose consensus as their mode of decision-making, which they did because of the positive experience they had had using consensus in Evergreen Association meetings.

In 2009, Wedgwood Community Church (WCC) began reviewing and updating its constitution and bylaws. During that process, the constitution committee decided to write the consensus model into the bylaws as the new way WCC would make decisions. The inspiration for switching to consensus was that the Evergreen Association, of which WCC is a member, was already using consensus. In January 2010, WCC's congregation affirmed their new constitution and bylaws by consensus, using this new decision-making method for the first time.

There were growing pains with this new method. Some church members wondered out loud what the point was. Some openly admitted to preferring the previous method using *Robert's Rules of Order*. Early on, with every important decision, the leaders of WCC had to spend more time explaining the consensus process to the congregation than the congregation spent using consensus to deliberate and decide on the issue in question. This sparked frustration that the whole thing was too bureaucratic and time-consuming. Even for the leaders, consensus felt clunky at times.

About a year in, things began to change. People became more familiar and comfortable with the process. Less time was spent explaining how it worked. Perhaps the clearest evidence that consensus was beginning to work was that the deliberation of issues took longer. Honest questions were asked and real dialogue ensued. There was a collective sense that, because we each fully owned every decision, we each needed a thorough understanding of the issue in question. People no longer asked rhetorical questions or made statements merely to vent or express ire, knowing that they would ultimately be outvoted anyway. Comments during deliberations seemed more genuine. When people raised concerns, it was more about how things could be improved, rather than just voicing disapproval and leaving it at that.

Of all the decisions made at WCC, consensus has worked best when it has been time to pass the yearly budget. Problems with line items in the proposed budget have surfaced through conversation. Efficient solutions have been created on the fly and applied. Consensus has empowered WCC's congregation to be better problem solvers, and consequently, everyone has a greater investment in the church's welfare and happenings.

One recent example is illustrative. Money had been taken out of WCC's endowment fund several times in 2019 to cover unforeseen expenses, and the endowment committee had carefully followed the protocol for dipping into the fund. However, when the congregation met to approve the budget, several people were concerned about that very protocol. More than one person did not want to move forward with affirming anything related to the 2020 budget until the endowment protocol was made more transparent and data was made more accessible to the congregation. Concerns about how WCC's finances were communicated internally also arose from this conversation. The leadership proposed concrete measures to address each of the concerns, at which time the congregation affirmed the budget. This example highlights the congregation's increased engagement, even at a detailed level, with the church's finances (usually not the most compelling topic for most people). It also shows how people can completely change their minds about an issue within a single meeting through the discussions and group problem-solving that are at the heart of consensus.

Such proficiency with consensus did not happen overnight. It was the result of long experience using it to tackle a variety of issues. I was on the initial committee that changed WCC's bylaws and introduced consensus. I was also a part of WCC's leadership team for four years after we started using consensus, and I am now pastor of WCC. I witnessed the evolution from growing pains and frustrations with the process to comfort and familiarity with it.

Using consensus in a church setting requires a good deal of trust among everyone involved. It demands that the leadership let go of some degree of control and let the process itself determine the outcome. That said, leaders still have an important role to play in consensus. They have to use their instincts and experience to know when the conversation needs to pause and dwell on a certain point, when it needs to move along, and when it needs to be postponed outright pending further research and clarification. Leaders must be prepared to facilitate meetings so that people's hard feelings and grave concerns are properly contextualized and channeled toward a decision to either pause, advance, or postpone the conversation.

It has been my observation that consensus has greatly improved the congregation's communication skills, their sense of buy-in to the church's ministries, and their ability to solve problems, even at a detailed level.

CHAPTER TWO
What Is Consensus?

Consensus is a way to make decisions as a group. It is defined as *rule by agreement*, and for faith communities, described as follows:

> We reach consensus when all of us are ready to live with the decision we are making. We do not all have to endorse it wholeheartedly, but we must all be ready to agree not to work or speak against the decision once it is made. Until we come to that point, our tasks are to share our ideas respectfully, listen to each other with open hearts, and find together what God wants us to do.

Consensus is fundamentally different from majority rule, drawing lots, dictatorship (rule by one person), or oligarchy (rule by a clique), other ways that groups make decisions. The most common method used today in the US, by far, is majority rule as delineated in *Robert's Rules of Order*.

The premise of majority rule is to make a decision that is approved by more than half the people who have a say, by voting. This is done by following a fairly strict set of rules. It is an orderly, efficient process, but too often, it cannot take the complexities of the decision into account, so the group must settle for the either/or choice that works for the majority of people. It also is designed to disregard the minority view, silencing voices that could help reach a better decision.

Consensus is a fundamentally different conceptual paradigm from majority rule. When it is done well, everyone feels heard and can live with the group's decision. This means you can make decisions that your whole community will embrace because their doubts and concerns have been addressed. It is more than the voice of the majority; it is the voice of all those who participate in making the decision.

The process for reaching true consensus is non-linear and complex. When a group is new to the process, it can feel messy and like more work than it is worth. Instead of two clear voices, one for and one against a decision, you have to listen to all the voices of the "murky middle." It takes time, and the discussion often wanders into unexpected issues, but the best answer to the matter in question might unexpectedly come from somewhere in the middle. When you listen to the thoughts and concerns of those in the middle, you may even find that the essence of the question changes. Without hearing the full range of voices in the meeting, you are left with an either/or choice that assumes there are only two perspectives.

If your group is committed to inclusivity and willing to persevere, you will eventually become comfortable with the messiness and appreciate the benefits of making decisions by consensus. With consensus, no decision is made, and no action is taken until everyone can live with it, even if they do not wholeheartedly support it. People often mistakenly think reaching consensus means everyone must wholeheartedly embrace every decision. It would be wonderful if that always happened, but most of the time, it does not. It is usually necessary for everyone to compromise at least a little to come to agreement. However, once you break out of the binary requirement of having to vote "yes" or "no," each person can consider giving in a little bit on some of the details in order to achieve something close to what they want. Best of all, when you get to agreement, everyone in the group is with you; there are no disgruntled losers.

Sometimes groups claim they are using consensus when they are not. This sometimes happens when a group's leaders want to rule by dictatorship or oligarchy but call their process consensus to get others to agree to use it. At other times, the facilitator does not understand the importance of following all the steps to reach true consensus and reverts to voting to get back into their comfort zone. Your group can avoid this kind of misappropriation by having everyone learn how true consensus works and commit to using it correctly. In fact, whatever decision-making process your group uses, you should all know the rules of the process and use them consistently.

For a group to reach true consensus, it must have a good facilitator who focuses on managing the process and has no personal stake in the outcome. A facilitator who has a personal interest in an issue cannot help but skew the process toward their desired outcome. This can be frustrating and disempowering for participants, and it misrepresents the process. Unfortunately, it takes only a few bad experiences with consensus done poorly to turn people off to the whole idea permanently. The facilitator needs to be completely committed to using consensus, even when the group is having trouble moving toward a decision. When the process bogs down, it is tempting to go back to familiar practices such as voting; it is part of the facilitator's job to lead the group through the impasse without abandoning the consensus process. (See Chapter 4 for more about the facilitator.)

Another essential component of a successful consensus process is time. It almost always takes longer to reach a decision by consensus than by voting. This is frustrating for a lot of people, especially at first. For consensus to work, your group needs to shift its collective attitude toward time and accept that it will take longer to get through the group's business. As you use consensus correctly, you may come to see the process itself and the extra time it takes as valuable to your community, not just the decisions that come out of the process. (See Chapter 5 for more about time.)

At its best, consensus brings us to Holy choices. Decisions made by a faith community using consensus are, in essence, given to the community by God. The ultimate test of the effectiveness of a faith-based consensus process is asking your group if the decision you have made is what God wants you to do. You may not always ask this out loud as you make each decision, but when the people in your group ask themselves this question, their inner answers should be "yes."

We have been called to share this process with you as a ministry. We hope it will help you and your congregation to treat each other justly, and with love and kindness with God as in Micah 6:8. We know from experience that choosing to use consensus is the best way to fulfill your desire to include God in all your work, both in the world and within your community.

How Evergreen Association Created Its Consensus Process

BY MARCIA J. PATTON

One Saturday in early autumn, I was one of a group of about thirty people who gathered to review bylaws for a new organization. Most of us had something else we would rather be doing that day than discussing rules and regulations, a task we imagined would be as dull as it sounded. Nonetheless, we came together to do just that. We came from congregations that had been members of American Baptist Churches of the Northwest, which had asked our congregations to leave their ranks and form our own regional association.

Earlier that year, a vision committee made up of two Asian Americans, two African Americans, and four Euro-Americans had come up with a name (Evergreen Association of American Baptist Churches) and a mission statement for the new organization.

They had also developed a structure based on ethnic caucuses, which was a significant departure from the usual Baptist association structure based on member churches' geographic locations. A "constituting convention" made up of representatives of all the member churches had met and affirmed the structure, name, and mission statement for the new organization. One of the next steps was writing the bylaws. The group that gathered that Saturday had come together to work on this task.

The structure that the constituting convention had approved required that there be three ethnic caucuses: Black, Asian, and Euro. (A Hispanic caucus was added a few years later.) There would be two representatives from each caucus on the executive committee; officers would serve two-year terms, with each office rotating through the caucuses; and for all meetings, the quorum required to do any business would include at least one representative from each caucus. As we reviewed the bylaws, we knew that they had to be based on this structure.

Our working group was a mix of clergy and laypeople representing all three ethnic caucuses. The majority of the participants were Euro-Americans, including some pastors. The Asian Americans in the group were all laypeople, and the African Americans were a mix of laypeople and ministers. We were giving our time to this new endeavor.

When we came to review the section called *Manner of Acting*, someone read out loud this draft text: "Majority will rule unless otherwise noted in these bylaws." These words were met with a disturbed, pregnant silence, unlike anything that had happened up to that point. When people finally began to speak again, it was with questions: "Is this the only option?" "Is there another way?" "What's an alternative?" "What if the minority has a significant question?" "Isn't this how we got here in the first place?" Eventually, we started to discuss possible answers to these questions and decided to look into other ways of doing business, particularly consensus. And so it began.

A few months later and after much more discussion, a group of about fifty people from many of the churches in the new association adopted bylaws (by consensus) that stated the association's manner of acting would be consensus. The bylaws included a definition of consensus and an addendum with some tools to use to reach consensus. Evergreen has used consensus to this day, with no indication that it ever intends to revert to majority rule.

Over almost two decades, we have come to recognize that one of the strongest parts of our process comes from our ethnic caucuses. Rather than trying to have a single conversation with twenty to twenty-five people at a board meeting or more than one hundred people at an annual meeting, we begin each meeting by reviewing the agenda and then break up into caucuses.

The ethnic caucuses create the space for conversations that would be difficult in the larger group. For example, the first time we discussed the financial support the association was receiving from member churches, each caucus was given a report of what every individual church was giving. The reality at the time was that the Euro caucus churches were giving the most financial support, by far, and the Black caucus churches were giving very little. When the large group reconvened, the Black caucus reported that they had discussed how little their churches were giving and they were going to do something about it. At that same meeting, as happened a lot in those early days, a white male participant asked, "Why are we meeting in these ethnic caucuses? I thought our goal was unity." The Black caucus answered his question with their report. If the discussion about financial contributions had happened only in the group as a whole, the Black caucus members most likely would have said nothing. If they had spoken, it would likely have been to defend their low level of support. Given the opportunity to talk frankly about the situation among themselves, they were able to focus their discussion on how they might be more supportive in the future. Giving the individual members of this group the space to speak freely and feel safe changed the conversation entirely.

There have been many other instances when a caucus has said something to the whole business meeting that made a difference, that individuals within the caucus would not have felt comfortable saying directly to the large group. Sometimes it has stopped a decision that wasn't fully thought through; other times it has helped us refine a decision to make it better. In every case, it was helpful to have a structure that allowed everyone to be engaged while feeling safe and heard.

CHAPTER THREE

Step by Step

Some people are reluctant to use consensus because they do not know how to get started and want a "road map." Unfortunately, there is no *Robert's Rules of Order* to tell you exactly what to do during every moment of the process. However, there is a general order of steps for effectively considering issues and making decisions by consensus, and a few rules that must be followed for the process to work. In this chapter, we describe the steps in a typical meeting using consensus. Most groups will need to customize their consensus process to fit their organizational structure and traditions. We offer this as a template for building a process that fits your group's needs.

The step-by-step process we describe here assumes that you are working with a large group (more than about twelve people) and need to divide into sub-groups to allow the depth of discussion needed to achieve true consensus. Some steps (e.g., the introduction of agenda items) may not be as important if the group is small enough to work as a whole all the way through the process. (See Step 5 below for more about sub-groups.)

Please note that we use the word *facilitator* to describe the person leading the process, as it comes closest to describing the function without giving preference to a name associated with any particular faith community. We encourage you to change the word to whatever works for your faith group. Also, when we write that the facilitator does something, there may be someone else in the group who can accomplish that task more easily than the facilitator, in which case we mean that the facilitator just needs to see that the task is done. It is perfectly all right for the facilitator to ask others to do some of the steps, though the facilitator must retain overall responsibility for the meeting.

1. Preparing for the Meeting

A meeting flows better if the people participating know what to expect. First of all, decide if you are going to conduct the meeting using consensus. If you choose to do this, commit to following the process through all the steps from start to finish. Do not try to hybridize your process, using some features of consensus and others of majority rule. We know from hard experience that this never works well.

There are two other important things to pay attention to before you convene a meeting. The obvious one is the agenda, and the second is the *grace margin*, described by Eric Law.[1] The grace margin is a space where everyone can feel safe doing the work they are called to do. For your group to function in the grace margin while conducting business, you need:

- Clear boundaries, which might include stating who is invited and perhaps who is not (e.g., children), where you are meeting and under what circumstances (e.g., if a meal will be provided), and who will be facilitating the meeting.
- Stated beginning and end times of the meeting.
- A written statement of the values on which you base your group activities. If your community already has a published statement of values, this is a great time to revisit it and make sure it reflects your community's current values.

The other important preparatory task is to carefully construct the agenda. It should include both topics for consideration and what action is associated with each item (e.g., announcement, report, initial presentation for discussion, intermediate discussion, or decision). It should also include an estimate of how long each item will take. These estimates are not meant to limit discussion or force decisions but just to give the group an idea of what to expect. People are less likely to go around and around on an issue if they know there is only so much time before the issue is set aside for another day. You might also include what is not going to be considered. For example, suppose people are worried that an issue is going to be decided prematurely at the meeting. In that case, you can state explicitly in the agenda that "no decision will be made at this meeting." Be sure to include opening and closing statements, readings, or prayers to foster a sense of unity.

We recommend that you always have a group build the agenda, or for a smaller meeting, at least a couple of people. Everyone participating in the meeting should know who is collecting agenda items for the meeting and the deadline for submitting them. In many Quaker meetings, a coordinating committee of representatives of all of the congregation's standing committees meets several days before each meeting for business. The clerk (leader of the congregation) facilitates this meeting (and also the meeting for business). Each committee rep tells of any agenda item(s) their committee wants to bring to the upcoming business meeting, including whether the item needs a discussion or a decision, or just an announcement or report. The clerk usually assembles the agenda then and there and asks for approval (by consensus) from the group. At Evergreen, the agenda for each executive committee meeting is drafted by the chair and then sent to the other members of the committee for review and approval before the meeting. The executive committee develops the agendas for each full board meeting and annual meeting in a similar manner.

If you are working with a group large enough to break into sub-groups for discussion, the agenda can include times and topics for sub-groups. For example, when Evergreen builds their business meeting agendas, they include the times that the caucuses will meet and what topics from the agenda of the main meeting the caucuses need to address. Since Evergreen's caucuses are standing groups that also have their own activities, they often have agenda items just for their group, such as planning a fund-raiser. Knowing in advance what they need to address as part of the larger group helps ensure that the caucuses devote enough time during caucus meetings to engage fully in making the decisions that define their community.

As you build a meeting's agenda, limit the number of issues you anticipate will require extended discussion. You can never be sure; sometimes an agenda item that seems simple unexpectedly engenders lengthy discussion. However, if you limit the number of known complex issues on the agenda, any unforeseen complications will have less impact on the meeting's overall success. If there is an essential or tender issue facing your group, let it be the only complex issue on the agenda. It's fine to add routine agenda items, especially if they are reports or announcements that do not require discussion or decisions but put the major issue "center stage" in the meeting, giving it the time and attention it deserves. If your community is facing multiple major decisions, give each one its own meeting, especially for the initial discussion and for reports from your sub-groups if you are using them. Share the agenda in advance with all participants. (See Appendix 1 for a sample agenda.)

Of course, if something urgent comes up at the last minute, agendas can change, but following a standard process when there are no emergencies helps everyone be on the same page. As you learn what the ensuing steps in this process are, you will see how important it is to prepare for the meeting in this way.

Lastly, make sure you have someone ready to take minutes. Ideally, your group will have one or two members who regularly take minutes and have agreed upon a standard format and style. Whether or not you have a designated recorder, taking good minutes is crucial to using consensus successfully; don't ever meet without making a record of the proceedings. Provide your recorder with a laptop and source of power or paper and pen. There must be no reason not to take minutes.

2. Getting Started

As with many activities, how you start a consensus-based business meeting can make a big difference in how the meeting proceeds and how satisfied you are with the results. You know that it is harder to get where you are going if you turn the wrong way when you leave home. To put it more positively, starting off in the right direction always makes the trip easier. This is also true of business meetings; as the saying goes, "Well begun is half done."[2]

When starting a consensus-based meeting, your goal is to bring your community together and help it feel connected to God. Unlike in a secular business meeting, you are not meeting on your own. As a faith community, God is already inherent in everything you do as a group. You help everyone remember this when you intentionally invite God to join you in your work. Also, as you do this together, you invite each participant to join with everyone else as a congregation to do God's work in the world (Matthew 18:20).

By long tradition, Quakers call their business sessions *meetings for worship with a concern for business*. To emphasize the worshipful nature of the process, they begin each business session with a time of silent worship ranging from a few moments to a half hour or more, depending on the congregation and the type of meeting. This helps them turn their attention away from secular matters, and as a congregation, become aware of the Divine participating in their business process. It also helps them loosen their attachment to their preconceived notions and open their minds to new possibilities. Quakers aspire to enter business meetings prepared to have their minds changed, acknowledging that they can corporately discern God's will best when they each let go a little of their need to be right. Starting a business meeting with worship helps remind everyone of this.

Of course, a time of silent worship is not the best meeting opener for most congregations. Your group may want to start with a prayer, a scripture reading, a liturgy, a song, or some combination of these. Do what is most comfortable in your faith tradition. Whatever ritual you use, the goal is to help participants know that they are together at home and that God is with them.

Resist the temptation to skip this step to "save time." Giving a full measure of attention to a gathering ritual helps your group feel that they are on familiar ground, even if the business process is a bit strange. Also, as we have said, a strong beginning can help you through rough spots later on. If your group bogs down mid-process, you may be glad to be able to refer back to the beginning and say, "as we prayed . . ." or "as our scripture reading at the beginning of the meeting reminded us. . . ."

3. Setting the Stage

Next, your facilitator outlines how the meeting will go, including presenting the agenda and stating how long the meeting is anticipated to last. It is helpful to be clear about the estimated length of the meeting at the beginning, to help participants relax about how long each item takes and not worry that the meeting will go significantly longer than they expect.

Until the group is familiar with the process, the facilitator should then summarize how consensus works, using words such as these:

> We reach consensus when all of us are ready to live with the decision we are making. We do not all have to endorse it wholeheartedly, but we must all be ready to agree not to work or speak against the decision once it is made. Until we come to that point, our tasks are to share our ideas respectfully, listen to each other with open hearts, and find together what God wants us to do.

This is also a good time to reaffirm whatever group norms your community has agreed to follow. If you do not already have some, we recommend establishing norms when you start using consensus. These might already be built into your community's work and ministry, but if not, creating and collectively affirming a set of behavioral guidelines will help people in your group work respectfully with others. You can find a variety of group norms on the internet, and we offer some that we have used with good effect in Appendix 4. Almost any norms will serve your group well, as long as the community affirms them and backs up the leadership when they need to be enforced.

If there are people in the meeting who are new to your community, it helps to spend a little extra time reviewing your group norms in detail and making sure that everyone understands them. When the whole community explicitly agrees to standards of behavior, individuals in the community are much more likely to abide by them. Also, if someone's behavior is problematic, you can use the norms to show them why their behavior is unacceptable without making it personal. (See Chapter 4 for more about group norms.)

4. Introducing Agenda Items

Everyone in the room needs to understand what questions are on the table and what to expect for each agenda item. Some agenda items may be reports or announcements or new issues being brought to the group for the first time. Some agenda items may address issues that the community has already begun discussing and are ready for either further discussion or a final decision. It is especially important to clarify what is expected if you are working with a large group that is going to break into sub-groups to discuss agenda items. It is counter-productive and discouraging to send people off to work on agenda items in sub-groups and have one sub-group come back with a *yes* or *no* when the rest of the sub-groups are just bringing back feedback or ideas. The agenda should be in writing, either posted on a board in the meeting room or handed out as printed copies (or both). The facilitator should also ask if there are any questions or clarifications needed about any item on the agenda before people divide up into sub-groups.

If you are working with a large group and sub-groups, there are two ways to work through your agenda items. One is to review the whole agenda with the large group, answer clarifying questions, and make sure all items are understood. Then the large group breaks into sub-groups that discuss all agenda items before re-assembling in the large group to go through the whole agenda again, with each sub-group sharing their input on all items. The other way is to introduce one agenda item at a time, answer any questions people have, break into sub-groups to discuss just that one item, and then get back together to share each sub-group's input on that item.

The first way is certainly more efficient, since you do not have to spend time moving around to form and re-form the large group and the sub-groups. It also allows sub-groups to allocate their time proportionally on what is most important to them, which often varies from one group to another. However, when you ask a sub-group to address many issues in one sitting, people sometimes lose focus as the topics multiply, and the last items on the list might not get enough attention. Especially if there is a complex or contentious issue facing the community, it is better to slow down the process. Have your sub-groups meet to discuss just that agenda item and then return to the large group to report. Of course, if you are a small group (or a group of Quakers) and don't need to break into sub-groups, you don't have to worry about this choice.

5. Setting Up Sub-Groups

When you are using consensus with a large group, it is usually good to use sub-groups to discuss issues in detail. This ensures that everyone has the opportunity to feel heard. For example, Evergreen's board meetings often have as many as fifty-five people participating, and participants at its association meetings can number in the hundreds. Making decisions by consensus with that many people is challenging, so Evergreen routinely uses their distinctive version of sub-groups, ethnic caucuses. Evergreen has four ethnic caucuses: Asian, Black, Euro, and Hispanic. Each individual attending an Evergreen meeting chooses the caucus they want to join, usually based on their personal ethnic identity, though occasionally (and particularly for clergy) based on their home congregation's dominant ethnicity. In addition, the Euro caucus often has enough participants at annual meetings that it subdivides further into even smaller groups for discussion, each of which reports back to the main Euro caucus group, so that the caucus as a whole can agree on a unified point of view regarding the issue in question and report that to the full association or board meeting. When the caucuses come back together to report, each caucus' point of view holds the same weight, regardless of the size of the caucus. This means that, even if the Euro caucus has seventy-five participants and the Hispanic caucus has two participants, each caucus' point of view carries equal weight in the full association or board meeting.

How you define your sub-groups depends on your community and the work you are doing. You might divide up randomly or in a variety of structured ways. Just be sure to choose your criteria for dividing up by consensus and using the criteria you choose consistently. Criteria to consider include:

- Is there a group or groups of people whose voice(s) may get lost if the sub-groups are created randomly?
- Does the outcome of this decision affect some people more than others?
- Is there a set of people who might overwhelm the other voices present because of their number?

Affirmative answers to any of these questions suggest that you may need to be deliberate in how you set up your sub-groups.

One effective approach is to set up sub-groups based on the affinity groups that already exist in your community. For example, Evergreen's Euro caucus often divides into four affinity groups: male clergy, female clergy, laywomen, and laymen, and some of these groups may subdivide again if they are too large to expedite discussion. Again, when they report back to the caucus, they each have an equal voice. This particular division helps moderate the clergy's voices and strengthens the laywomen's voices; everyone is heard more clearly.

Resist the urge to make all sub-groups the same size. It doesn't matter how big or small each group is, as long as each is given an equal voice in the larger meeting. Also, be careful not to fall into the trap of thinking every sub-group must have the same demographic profile as the large group. For example, if 20 percent of the people in your group are women, you might be tempted to make sure that 20 percent of all your sub-groups are women. This does not work because those in the minority in the large group remain in the minority, making it difficult for their voices to be heard. Sub-groups based on affinity allow every demographic element of your large group to have a voice in the overall discussion.

Quakers do not generally break up into small groups to discuss issues during business meetings, regardless of how many people are participating. Instead, they have developed a unique business process over the past 360 years, based on referring virtually every issue to a standing or ad hoc committee. The committee is empowered by the meeting as a whole to meet as many times as necessary and to gather whatever outside resources are needed, to fully understand the issue. Then it brings a recommendation to the meeting for business. If the meeting does not accept the recommendation by consensus, the issue is returned to the committee with feedback and questions. This process is repeated until the committee brings a recommendation that the meeting as a whole can accept. We do not recommend that groups new to consensus use this method. For it to work, the community needs to be experienced and confident using consensus and have well-established and well-functioning committees tending to the full range of the community's responsibilities.

6. Discussing Each Agenda Item

When discussing an agenda item, whether in a large group or in sub-groups, the goal is to ensure that everyone who wants to contribute to the discussion can do so. Everyone must feel welcome to address the topic at hand, so that one point of view does not dominate the discussion. We recommend using Mutual Invitation or a similar communication tool. These tools help ensure that only one person speaks at a time and that comments are relevant to the topic rather than personal diatribes or attacks. In addition, group and sub-group facilitators can use these tools to ensure that quiet people get to speak, and verbose people speak only once or twice. (See Chapter 4 for more about communication tools.)

Although it is the facilitator's job to ensure that everyone has the opportunity to be heard and understood and that no one dominates the conversation, it is the whole group's responsibility to support the facilitator in doing this. This means that everyone should be on the alert for the person or faction that won't stop repeating their point of view, that interrupts or makes hurtful remarks to people voicing divergent views, or that objects to a decision while refusing to give their reasons. These are all forms of bullying, and the best way to curb this behavior is to have everyone in the group committed to stopping it whenever it starts.

When there is a new issue on the agenda in a large group meeting, the facilitator invites people to ask clarifying questions and makes sure that the questions are answered. They then instruct the sub-groups to discuss the issue and report back at the next large group meeting, which could be in a few minutes or a few days, depending on the complexity of the issue, the constraints of the other items on the agenda, and the time limits of the meeting.

For an agenda item that has already been discussed in sub-groups, the facilitator asks one member of each sub-group to report on that group's collective point of view regarding the issue. Every sub-group has an equal voice in presenting its view, regardless of its relative size. Then the facilitator opens the item for further general discussion, which is inevitably informed by the sub-groups' presentations. Sometimes one sub-group offers an idea that the other sub-groups need to discuss, to be sure that everyone's voice is heard regarding this idea. When this happens, the facilitator refers the agenda item back to the sub-groups, and any pending decision is set aside until they can meet again.

Including estimated times for each item on the agenda helps in this situation. If some people are reluctant to set aside an issue in order to have a new idea related to it discussed in sub-groups, the facilitator can refer to the time estimates for agenda items. They can also remind participants that the most important part of the consensus process is hearing every voice to find a solution everyone can live with, no matter how long it takes. There are rare situations when setting aside an issue for further discussion in the future is not the best practice. Once in a while, an issue will capture the meeting's attention so deeply that it needs to be discussed at length right then. When this occurs, the facilitator should ask if the group wants to set aside other items on the agenda to give this one item the time it needs. Only the group as a whole should make the decision to dramatically change the agenda in the middle of a meeting, never the facilitator alone.

7. Assessing Progress toward a Decision

This part of the process can feel quite messy. Throughout the discussion, the facilitator needs to have a good idea of what people are thinking about and how they feel. Quakers call this the *sense of the meeting*. For the facilitator to maintain this sense, they need to pause the discussion periodically and either summarize what they think are the group's points of view and identify the outstanding issues or ask respected community members in the room to share their perceptions. If the facilitator asks for input from others, they still need to articulate the sense of the meeting to the whole group, incorporating the guidance of those who have spoken.

After summarizing their sense of the meeting, the facilitator should ask for confirmation that they have stated an accurate reflection of the group's position. If they have, the facilitator then offers guidance for the next step in the process. If there isn't agreement, the facilitator can let the discussion continue for a while longer to allow more clarity to emerge. If it seems that the outstanding issues are insurmountable, they can send the agenda item back to the sub-groups for further deliberation.

One way to get a more detailed understanding of the group's progress toward a decision is to have everyone indicate, by a show of fingers, where they are on the following scale of levels of consensus. Each person in the group may:

1. Have whole-hearted support for the decision.

2. Have slight reservations about the decision but will support it.

3. Have some reservations about the decision but will support it.

4. Have serious reservations about the decision but will support it.

5. Have major problems with the decision and will not support it.

6. Have one or more questions or concerns about the decision that, if addressed, may allow them to support it.

This is not simply a matter of "yes" or "no;" don't think of it as a *straw vote*. (Ideally, never say or think the word *vote* while using consensus.) Unless the fingers that go up around the room are mostly ones and twos, your group is not ready to make a decision.

Once everyone has held up fingers, the facilitator should check in with those who are at two and three to make sure they are really ready to support the decision. If anyone is at five, the group can't move forward until their concerns are addressed. If one person is at four, they may be willing to *stand aside*, as the Quakers say, and let the group move forward to a decision. However, if more than one person is at four, the group needs to address their concerns also. You cannot reach true consensus while some participants still have serious reservations or major problems with a decision; doing this kind of feedback exercise helps you see what questions and concerns may be blocking you. (See Chapter 4 for more about levels of consensus.)

8. Confirming the Decision

When the facilitator gets confirmation from the group that their perception of the group's point of view is correct, they should state the proposed decision as simply as possible, and the recorder should write it down. If there has been significant discussion of concerns leading up to the decision, make sure that the recorder includes a summary of the concerns in the minute, as well as the actual decision made. If everyone in the group supports the decision as stated by the facilitator, and if the group approves minutes at future meetings, the facilitator then moves on to the next agenda item.

If the group approves minutes as decisions are made (highly recommended for groups new to consensus), the group waits while the recorder writes a minute stating the decision and summarizing the key reasons for it. The recorder then reads the minute and asks for approval, which the group must give by consensus. If anyone has an objection to the content of the minute, it is re-written and re-read until the group can approve it. This might necessitate returning the issue to sub-groups if the decision was not as close as the facilitator thought it was.

It has been our experience that, regardless of the group's usual practice regarding approving minutes, certain decisions are big enough to warrant having the minute written and read at the point of decision. This ensures that everyone is aware of the actual decision they have made and that the issue does not have to be revisited at a future meeting.

9. Closing the Meeting

After all agenda items have been addressed, it is important to have a focused close to the meeting. Do your best to close the meeting with the same intention you had when opening it. This helps participants move from the meeting environment back into the secular world. Your tradition may have a common ritual for ending gatherings, such as a benediction, prayer, or song. Quakers return to silent worship for a few moments and then either stand and hold hands in a circle or stay seated and shake hands with the people near them.

The closing of your business meetings should include a brief summary of the work the group has just done, an encouraging word for re-entering the world, and assurance that God goes with each person.

The summary should include only the decisions made, the issues referred to sub-groups, and the new issues introduced. Do not elaborate or retell how you got there. If you have reached a major decision after long deliberation, by all means celebrate that, but don't neglect to mention other major topics that came up in the meeting.

Offer encouragement to participants for whatever may be next for them. This helps people mentally disengage from the issues discussed in the meeting and turn their attention fully to whatever awaits them outside the meeting space. When a facilitator ends a meeting with a simple dismissal, such as "Well, I think that's it for today," many people leave the meeting feeling like they left the car running in the garage and came into the house. The car is out of sight but can't be put out of mind because it is not "parked." Speaking briefly about how participants will go forward from the meeting helps people anticipate what might be next in their lives, including when you might be together again.

It is also important to remind participants that God goes with them and that they are not alone in the work they are doing in the world, whatever that may be. For some congregations, this might include a reminder of concerns the community has beyond that meeting's business, such as those who are ill or grieving.

Just a few sentences are sufficient, along with whatever closing ritual is familiar to your community. The important parts are to be intentional and make sure to take enough time to do it well. This helps people return to their sense of your congregation as home, so they leave the meeting feeling part of the community. If your group does not have a parting ritual, we recommend that you create one for use, at least, at the end of business meetings.

UFM Accepts Same-Sex Marriage

BY DR. DORSEY GREEN AND NORA J. PERCIVAL

Dr. Dorsey Green is a former clerk of Friends Committee on National Legislation, a national Quaker organization that lobbies Congress for peace, justice, and environmental stewardship. She is also a former clerk of University Friends Meeting, Nora's home congregation.

The marriage ritual at most Quaker meetings is rather different from the traditional American wedding, specifically in that the couple is married by the whole congregation. When a couple wants to get married, they formally request to be married "under the care of the meeting." A clearness committee (a small group of people who know the couple) meets with them one or more times. The committee then makes a recommendation to the business meeting to take the marriage under its care. Once the business meeting approves the recommendation, there is a special meeting for worship during which the couple says their vows to each other and those who wish to orally bless the marriage also speak. At the end of the worship time, everyone present signs the marriage certificate.[3] In this way, the community takes collective responsibility to support the marriage.

University Friends Meeting (UFM) began to consider taking same-sex marriages under its care in 1981, when two women who were respected, active members of the community requested to be married under the care of the meeting. This led UFM to begin seeking unity on using the word *marriage* for same-sex as well as heterosexual unions. Quakers use the word *unity* rather than *consensus* to emphasize that their process is focused on corporate discernment of God's will rather than simply agreement of all people present, as with secular consensus. As is so often the case with Quaker process, it took a long time to find unity on this issue; it was not fully resolved until 1992.

Four stages led to the final decision to approve same-sex marriage. The first stage, which began in 1977, was characterized by excitement at the increasing number of lesbian and gay people joining the community. As members of the meeting began to get to know queer people, there was a general interest in accepting and supporting this marginalized group. There were study hours about homosexuality and informal conversations happening all around the meeting.

When the two women's request for marriage came to the meeting, the community began to consider it. Some members formed a gay/lesbian support group called *Lavender and Grey* that met regularly and included many straight allies. However, although there was widespread support for the two women and for taking their relationship under the care of the meeting, there was not unity to call the relationship a *marriage*. After three business meetings with this as the main item on the agenda, the community agreed to hold a "celebration of commitment under the care of the meeting." (Without realizing it at the time, this was probably the first time in the US that a Quaker meeting took a same-sex relationship under its care.)

The second stage was the golden age of acceptance. It began with the celebration of commitment for these two women. The community was happy to celebrate and proud of itself. There was a second celebration of commitment for a gay couple in 1985 and a third celebration of commitment for a lesbian couple in 1990. In 1986, Oversight Committee (equivalent to a pastoral care committee) asked the community to consider using the term *marriage* for committed same-sex relationships. The community formed small discussion groups to talk about the meaning of marriage and how to care for all committed relationships. Each group met several times. There were no decisions to be made by these discussion groups, which made it easier for participants to speak with open hearts and have their words received tenderly. As a result, people felt more connected to each other and aware of the importance of supporting all committed couples. Some people in the community were overt in their opposition to same-sex marriage, but they did not participate in the discussion groups.

The third stage overlapped with the second stage and was characterized by open opposition. In 1987, the community held a special meeting to consider same-sex relationships, at which hurtful words were said. One member's behavior was particularly egregious when he showed a painting of a pregnant heterosexual woman as an example of what God intended for humans. Sadly, no one challenged him or any of the other hurtful speech. Soon after, someone submitted a letter to be read at a meeting for business, stating that same-sex relationships differ from heterosexual ones and the community should stop talking about the issue. It was authored by a founding member of UFM and signed by a number of other people who supported him. Several signers later said that they didn't necessarily agree with the author but respected him enough to sign his letter. That same year, a gay man's membership application was held over for an extra month because of one person's clear homophobic beliefs. As before, there was no overt challenge from the community as a whole.

In 1988, Oversight recommended that UFM not perform any marriages or celebrations of commitment for any couples, at least for a few months. This hiatus actually lasted until 1990, when the community approved a celebration of commitment for a lesbian couple. At the same business meeting, the community sought but did not find unity to use the term *marriage* for only heterosexual couples and therefore agreed not to use it for any couples until there was unity regarding the use of the term. For the next two years, all unions taken under the care of UFM were called *celebrations of commitment*. Several members of the congregation left during this time to join a different Quaker meeting. Some of those who left, including both queer and straight Friends, said that they could no longer deal with the tension and pain at UFM.

The fourth stage overlapped with the third stage. It started when the community began to focus more on the "good order of Friends." (See Chapter 4 and Appendix 3 for more about the good order of Friends.) Specifically, the group began to deal directly with behavior that was hurtful, mean, or homophobic. This shift began when a new clerk (administrative leader) was appointed by the community in 1989.[4] He brought a deeply spiritual leadership style that helped the community focus more on its shared spirituality as a community and less on its differences. He was followed in 1991 by a clerk who focused on educating the community about good Quaker business process. These leaders were able to shift the direction of the discernment process toward seeking God's will for the group.

There were still instances of bigotry and mean-spirited behavior. For example, three signatories of the anti-gay marriage letter took down several pictures that were part of an art show and harassed the office manager when she tried to stop them. They defended their actions by saying the scenes depicted gay men. However, the meeting's leadership reacted strongly this time, condemning the act and publicly reprimanding the men. This marked the beginning of public criticism of anti-gay behavior, and it helped change the tenor of the discernment process. Incidences of homophobic and personally hurtful speech in business meetings continued but now were openly challenged, both by the targets of the malicious behavior and by Oversight. The mood was changing; people were no longer willing to "go along to get along" to keep the peace.

In 1991, the business meeting devoted an hour at one monthly meeting to hearing people's pain and another hour at the following meeting to talking about what the community needed to do to heal. The following year, the community held a workshop on finding unity, and a large percentage of community members participated. It was a heart-opening experience of seeking God's leading for the group. The deepening spirituality in worship and business meetings, the two hours of sitting with each other in pain and intention to heal, and the workshop all contributed to helping the community engage in an entirely different way with the issue of naming committed relationships.

That same year, a heterosexual couple asked to have their relationship taken under the care of the meeting. In this couple's letter of request, they asked if it was time for UFM to begin allowing couples to call it *marriage* again. During the discussion of their request, it became clear that there was unexpected unity for all couples to call their commitments under the care of the meeting by any name they chose. The business meeting approved a minute stating simply that any couple may name their union whatever they want and the community would take the relationship under its care.

Unbeknownst to each other, the clerk and the recording clerk (equivalent to a secretary) called people whom they knew opposed same-sex marriage and who had not been at the business meeting. In every case, the people who were called accepted that the community had finally decided; in some cases, they were relieved.

When the first two women asked to be married under the care of the meeting in 1981, the community's discernment process was thorough and in good order. There wasn't unity to call the relationship a marriage, but there was unity to hold the commitment celebration. Unfortunately, after that, the community allowed a few members to interfere with the community's discernment process, and these people were emboldened by the community's discomfort with holding people accountable for hurtful behavior. This is a vulnerability that many groups using consensus share. We must remember to hold people accountable when they behave in ways that are destructive to unity, in order to support our community's health and facilitate good decision-making.

Notes

1. Rev. Dr. Eric H. F. Law, *Inclusion: Making Room for Grace* (St. Louis, MO: Chalice Press, 2000), https://www.kscopeinstitute.org/free-resources.

2. Aristotle, *Politics*, Greece, 4th century BC.

3. If legal documents need to be signed by an officiant, the clerk of the meeting signs on behalf of the community.

4. Most Quaker meetings appoint clerks and other officers of the congregation for terms of two or three years. As a result, many different people hold these positions over the course of time.

CHAPTER FOUR
The Facilitator

The person directing the consensus process for your group can be called by many names. We use *facilitator* in this book, as it comes closest to describing the function without giving preference to a name associated with any particular faith community. If your community leader is called a clerk, moderator, president, chair, pastor, or something else, replace *facilitator* with that name as you read this chapter.

The facilitator's role is crucial to the quality of both the consensus process and the resulting decisions. A good facilitator can lead a group through the most complex issues to clear and inclusive decisions. A poor facilitator can ruin the experience for some or all participants and make it impossible for the group to reach authentic consensus.

The role of the facilitator is to:

- Ensure that the agenda is set.
- Move the agenda forward.
- Initiate and manage the use of communication tools.
- Encourage quiet people to share.
- Encourage verbose people to speak less.
- Restrain the tyranny of the one.
- Reflect collective points of view.

- Stop all speech intended to hurt others.
- Protect vulnerable groups.
- Remain neutral to the outcome.
- Ask for help when needed.

Ensure that the Agenda Is Set

Creating a good agenda is an important first step toward having a successful consensus-based meeting. As the facilitator, your first job is to ensure that the agenda includes both the necessary topics for consideration and what action is associated with each item (e.g., announcement, report, initial presentation for discussion, intermediate discussion, or decision). It should include an estimate of how long each item will take, not to limit discussion or force decisions, but just to give the group an idea of what to expect. Also, as the facilitator, you can use these time estimates during the meeting to limit discussion when it is wandering off the topic or becoming adversarial.

You might also include what is not going to be considered. For example, if people are worried that an issue is going to be decided prematurely, you can state explicitly in the agenda that "no decision will be made at this meeting." If you are working with a group large enough to break into sub-groups for discussion, the agenda can include times and topics for sub-groups. Be sure to include an opening and closing statement, reading, or prayer in your agenda; this helps reinforce the sense that everyone is working together as a community. (See Appendix 1 for a sample agenda.)

Whenever possible, have a group build the agenda, or for a smaller meeting, have at least a couple of people work together to create it. As the facilitator, you need to participate in developing the agenda, but you should not build it all by yourself if you can avoid it. This helps diffuse any tendency to think that the facilitator is including or excluding possible agenda items for personal reasons. To further ensure that everyone feels included, create a standard process through which people can request to add an item to the agenda. Make sure everyone knows how to make such a request and what the deadline is for submitting it.

The specific way your group sets agendas will be determined somewhat by the general practices in your community. For example, in many Quaker congregations, the agendas for business meetings are created by a coordinating committee made up of representatives of all of the congregation's standing committees. In other organizations, an executive committee or council of elders might use a similar process. The important thing is to ensure that all community members have the opportunity to bring issues to the business meeting.

Limit the number of issues on a single agenda that you anticipate will require extended discussion. You can never be sure, but don't plan for a meeting to include many long discussions. If there is a really important or tender issue facing your group, let it be the only complex issue on the agenda. If your community is facing multiple major decisions, give each one its own meeting, especially for the initial discussion and for reports from subgroups. (See Chapter 3, Step 1 for more about agendas.)

Move the Agenda Forward

The facilitator's principal work is to keep the meeting moving through the agenda while helping participants make good decisions and encouraging everyone to participate in the decision-making process. This means that, as the facilitator, you need to keep your attention on the participants, the items you need to address, and the time. This can be a lot to focus on all at once; it's fine to seek help with these tasks. Some facilitators ask someone else to act as a timekeeper. Others ask someone to help keep track of people who wish to speak. As long as you, as the facilitator, retain overall responsibility and authority for the running of the meeting, it is perfectly appropriate to delegate parts of your task. Ideally, you don't want to tarry too long or rush through any single agenda item. Learning to manage the flow of the meeting well takes practice. Give yourself a chance to do it imperfectly a few times; it gets easier as you do it more.

Use Communication Tools and Group Norms

As the facilitator, the quality (not the content) of communications and interactions in the meeting is in your care. To do this part of the job well, you need a full box of tools, such as Mutual Invitation and RESPECT guidelines. These tools are remarkably useful at all stages of consensus-based meetings. You will find them particularly helpful when one person or faction is bullying another person or the meeting as a whole by repeating their point of view, interrupting, or insulting people voicing divergent views.

Mutual Invitation helps people listen and talk to each other. Especially in these days of virtual meetings, your group might benefit from using Mutual Invitation, where one person shares and then invites someone else to share. That person can share, pass for now and ask to have the group come back to them later in the discussion, or pass completely because they have nothing to share on the subject. Then they invite another person to share, until everyone who wants to has had a chance to speak.

RESPECT Guidelines[1] are a set of group norms presented as a mnemonic. "R" reminds people to take *responsibility* for what they say and feel without blaming others. "E" reminds people to use *empathetic* listening. "S" reminds people to be *sensitive* to differences in communication styles. "P" encourages people to *ponder* what they hear and feel before they speak. "E" encourages people to *examine* their own assumptions and perceptions. "C" reminds people to share *constructively* for the community's benefit and to maintain a safe space for everyone. "T" suggests that people *trust* the process. (See Appendix 3 for more about RESPECT Guidelines.)

Quakers have long professed to do business according to the *good order of Friends*, or GOOF. One description of this is to *Gather* to address community concerns as a community; *Open* to the Spirit working through the people as a group, including opening to the possibility of having one's mind changed during the discussion; *Observe* how the sense of the meeting evolves as people share their thoughts; and have *Faith* that God is working through you and will lead your group to the best decision for your community.

Sometimes group norms can be created at the beginning of a meeting. At the first meeting of one working group that Marcia was part of, the group made a simple list of their norms. They included: commit to working through mistakes in a relational way; be open to others' perspectives; be kind, have grace, and give others grace; and take space, make space. At the beginning of each meeting, they reviewed this list and asked if it needed to be amended. (See Appendices 2 and 3.)

There are many communication tools and group norms available. We offer these because we have used them successfully in our meetings, but if you already have tools or norms that work for your group, use them instead. Whatever tools you use, become as familiar as possible with how they work. Participants may suggest which tools your group should use, but it is up to you as the facilitator to put them into action when and how you think best. Take the time to study how the tools work and what the norms mean. The more familiar you are with them, the better able you will be to guide the conversation well.

Whatever guidelines you choose to use, don't assume people know them; review them at every meeting. It helps to make this a regular part of the opening sequence of your meetings. You may also need to review during the meeting how the tool(s) are meant to be used or what norms you have accepted as a group, if people begin to drift into more adversarial communication modes.

Encourage Quiet People to Share

One of the most important reasons to know and use good communication tools is to give people who tend to be quiet the opportunity to express their points of view. The importance of this varies with the nature of the decision you are considering, but the best practice is to assume that you need to give everyone, even the "wallflowers," the chance to speak on every topic. When your group is facing a major decision, it is critical to hear from everyone in order to reach true consensus. Some people consistently need encouragement to share what they are thinking; it is your job as the facilitator to offer that encouragement. Don't assume that a person who hasn't spoken necessarily agrees or disagrees with a particular point of view. Get them to share their point of view, so they know they have been heard, and everyone else knows where they stand. Good communication tools can help you do this.

If someone in your group consistently declines to speak to the group, even when invited, ask someone they trust to meet with them before the meeting. Have this person get their view privately and ask for permission to share it with the group, either by speaking it on their behalf or reading a written statement. This is also a way to include the views of someone who cannot attend a meeting in person due to health or personal concerns.

The goal is to make sure that everyone's voice is heard. This informs the group's decisions with all the wisdom available, and it also reinforces for everyone that, in your community, no one's point of view is excluded.

Encourage Verbose People to Speak Less

Just as some people need to be encouraged to speak up, other people need to be encouraged not to dominate the conversation or repeat themselves. Good communication tools can also help this situation. As the discussion progresses, if the communication process begins to devolve, do not hesitate to remind people of the guidelines you set at the beginning of the meeting. You can also use time to your advantage in working with verbose people. When you start to discuss a particular issue, you can tell the group that you have so many minutes and so many people in the room, which means that each person has about so many minutes to speak to this issue. Many people are better at watching time for themselves when given these parameters.

In addition, do not hesitate to address an individual's behavior if it is damaging the group process. You can gently interrupt someone who is rambling on or excessively repeating their point. Ask the person to make their point in a sentence or thank them for the point they have already made and call on someone else. If they continue to talk, stand next to them so they know you are supporting them, and then interrupt them again and call on someone else to speak.

If you are concerned before the meeting that a particular person will dominate the conversation, ask someone they trust, who is familiar with the communication tools you will be using, to sit next to the person and help them with a touch on the arm or other signal when they have said enough. You could also have a conversation before the meeting with a particularly verbose person to share your concerns and ask the person to agree to keep their remarks brief. Offer to help them live up to their agreement and tell them what cues you will give them when they need to stop talking.

As with quiet people, the goal is to make sure that everyone's voice is heard. Keeping verbose people from dominating the process allows all the wisdom available to come into the conversation. It also reinforces for everyone that, in your community, no one's point of view is more important than any other.

Restrain the Tyranny of the One

Every now and then, someone wants to block a decision but doesn't want to give a reason. When this happens, pause the discussion and refer your group back to the description of consensus:

> We reach consensus when all of us are ready to live with the decision we are making. We do not all have to endorse

it wholeheartedly, but we must all be ready to agree not to work or speak against the decision once it is made. Until we come to that point, our tasks are to share our ideas respectfully, listen to each other with open hearts, and find together what God wants us to do.

Emphasizing the last sentence, remind everyone that your work at this point is to help the whole group figure out what God wants you to do. If everyone cannot share their concerns, the group cannot move forward. If you have the time in the meeting, take a break to give everyone a few minutes to consider their point of view. If your agenda is too full, set aside the issue until a future meeting. Don't let the "tyranny of the one" stop the process or force a premature decision. This would be reverting to autocracy; it also undermines everyone's faith in consensus as a process.

Reflect the Collective Point of View

A big part of your job as the facilitator is to listen carefully to the conversation. When it seems that people are approaching agreement, either on the whole question or on one aspect of it, pause the discussion to ask the group if your perception is accurate. Quakers speak of this as seeking the *sense of the meeting*, meaning either the general direction in which the group's collective attitude is moving or a decision that seems to be emerging.

As appropriate, repeat words you have heard spoken that summarize what you are sensing. If someone has made a point with particular clarity, acknowledge them as well as their words. Others in the group will remember how they felt when that person was speaking, which will help them gauge how much they agree with the point.

Be careful how you phrase your summary statement. Avoid sounding like you are challenging people to disagree, such as by saying, "It sounds to me that we agree to this; will anyone speak against it?" or "Does anyone have further concerns about it?"

This can make people feel like they must either instantly voice a coherent objection or be quiet and accept your assessment, even if they are not ready to agree. Instead, try to frame your summary more openly, such as by saying, "The last four people have spoken in favor of this; we need to hear from someone who has a question or concern." Be sure to give people a few moments to consider what you have said and formulate their authentic responses.

You can also use this "pause for summary" technique to bring up remaining disagreements if the group seems stuck on one or a few aspects of the issue. Try to articulate the essence of the opposing points of view, such as by saying, "We have heard many concerns about this issue (list them if you can), yet it seems that we still have these two (or however many) conflicting points of view. Shall we send this question back to the sub-groups for further discussion?" It is always better to send an issue back to sub-groups than to continue talking in circles in the large group. If your group is too small to have sub-groups, suggest that you set aside the issue until a future meeting, and ask people to think about their concerns and discuss them informally with each other in the meantime. (Quakers call this getting the *sense of the parking lot*.)

Measure How Close You Are to Consensus

When you sense that the group is nearing agreement on an issue or one part of an issue, pause the discussion and ask people to indicate, by a show of fingers, where they are on the following scale of levels of consensus. Each person in the group may:

1. *Have whole-hearted support for the decision.* Ideally, this is where you want everyone in the group to be on all decisions. Realistically, a large majority of people need to be here for you to consider your group near consensus on any issue.

2. *Have slight reservations about the decision but will support it.* People will often choose this if they aren't 100 percent in favor of the decision but are okay with it. If you have a large

majority of people at one and the rest of the group at two, ask the people at two to confirm that they are ready to agree to the decision.

3. ***Have some reservations about the decision but will support it.*** If you have people at three, ask them to share their reservations and discuss them fully in the group. If you can address them satisfactorily, the threes will become twos and ones.

4. ***Have serious reservations about the decision but will support it.*** Quakers call this position *standing aside*. It means the person is unable to support the decision but does not need to block it. If one person is at four, it may be okay for the group to move forward to a decision (with gratitude for the person standing aside). However, if more than one person is at four, you need to address their concerns before proceeding. In any case, it is important to listen carefully to the concerns of even one person at four. They may just be the one who hears something God is trying to tell your group that others are not hearing.

5. ***Have major problems with the decision and will not support it.*** If you have even one person in your group at five, you must set aside further discussion of the issue until you find out why they can't support the decision. If they do not want to share their reasons with the group at that time, ask a respected member of your community to meet with them privately, or invite them to submit their objections to the facilitator in writing. You cannot move forward to consensus when one or more participants have serious reservations or major problems with a decision.

6. ***Have one or more questions or concerns about the decision that, if addressed, may allow them to support it.*** People at six are not ready to assess their level of consensus. They still need more information or understanding before they can deter-

mine their position. When their questions and concerns are addressed, they may move to ones or twos, but until then, they block consensus as much as people at five do.

Reassure participants that it is not simply a matter of "yes" or "no," and avoid calling it a "straw vote." (Ideally, never say the word *vote* while using consensus.) Unless the fingers that go up around the room are mostly ones and twos, find out what questions people need to have addressed before they can move forward. Listen to the group's murmur and watch people's body language to see if they are feeling pushed to think in these terms too soon. If you sense reluctance, just let it go and call on the next person who wants to speak.

This is just one method for assessing a group's readiness for consensus. If it doesn't suit your group, adapt it or use another method. What is most important is that you monitor the progress of the group toward consensus.

Stop All Speech Intended to Hurt Others

Even when you have clearly stated the guidelines for communication, someone may say something hurtful to others in the group, or to people outside the group. As the facilitator, it is part of your job to stop such speech. It is necessary and appropriate for you to immediately interrupt someone being hurtful. Be careful to do so respectfully, to ensure that you do not inadvertently hurt the speaker in the process of stopping their hurtful speech. If you are not comfortable confronting the person, ask for help from others in the meeting. If a person does not stop speaking hurtfully, ask them to leave. It helps to ask a well-respected member of your group to accompany them and help them understand, outside the meeting room, why they had to leave.

In rare instances, a person will neither stop speaking hurtfully nor leave. This happened once in Nora's meeting. One person was speaking at great length and maligning specific individuals in the group. The facilitator asked her to stop, but she refused. Then a trusted friend of hers sat beside her and asked her to stop; she refused. Then the whole group stood up in silence (a traditional Quaker response in this situation) to indicate that they did not accept her behavior; she continued to speak. The facilitator then told her she would have to leave, but she refused to do so. Finally, the facilitator announced that, in the face of this uncontrollable disturbance, they were ending the meeting, and everyone should leave, which they did. Most meetings should never have to resort to this type of action, but when all else fails, stopping hurtful speech is more important than anything else.

Protect Vulnerable Groups

Another important part of your job as the facilitator is to protect vulnerable groups. Depending on the makeup of the community, this might include laity, women, a particular ethnic group, immigrants, young people, or older people. Context is everything in defining people's vulnerability. Do not make assumptions about it; even a group that usually has authority is occasionally vulnerable in the context of a particular issue. For example, one or a few men serving on a committee focused on women in ministry and made up mostly of women might be vulnerable to coercion by the majority gender.

Think about your community's population and observe the power dynamics among your community members in informal settings. This can help you anticipate who may feel vulnerable in the more formal setting of a business meeting. Do not be shy about analyzing your community in terms of factions. They are intrinsic to group dynamics, and the more you pay attention to them, the less likely they are to be divisive.

Once you identify a vulnerable group, pay particular attention to their needs in the group process, making sure they have the opportunity to participate without intimidation. One of the best ways to protect vulnerable groups is to base your sub-groups on your community's natural affinity groups. This offers everyone a safe place to share their thoughts without fear of being criticized or shut down. (See Chapter 3, Step 5 for more about sub-groups.)

Remain Neutral to the Outcome

Often, the hardest part of facilitating a consensus process is maintaining a neutral point of view. This is crucial, as you must remain disinterested in the outcome of a discussion in order to pay close enough attention to the process to be sure that all voices are being heard. It is like being a moderator at a debate; your role is to see that the process is conducted and time is managed in accordance with the group's expectations, and no more. There is no room in the facilitator's role for your opinions.

While you are facilitating a meeting, if you feel that you must voice a point of view on a particular issue, ask someone else to act as the facilitator while discussing that issue. If possible, move out of the facilitator's chair and let the other person occupy it while you participate in the discussion. As soon as that particular discussion ends, return to the facilitator's chair and take up your duties again. This helps ensure that the consensus process will continue unimpeded. It also sends a powerful message to the group that, as the facilitator, you are impartial and can be trusted to support the process for everyone.

Ask for Help When You Need It

Especially when your group is new to consensus, you may need to ask someone from outside the group to facilitate your meetings. Find someone who is familiar with your community and experienced in using consensus, but not affiliated with any faction within your group. Even after your group becomes adept at using consensus, you may want to bring in an outside facilitator for a major decision that stirs strong feelings in everyone in the group. If you are going to use an outside facilitator, it is far better to start doing this at the beginning of the discussion.

Even if you do not need someone else to facilitate, you may need help in other ways. This will happen more when you are new to facilitating, but even the most experienced facilitators need help sometimes. If you know that a complex issue on the agenda is likely to challenge you as a facilitator, ask ahead of time for a trusted colleague to offer you guidance through the meeting. If you begin to feel uncertain during a meeting, pause the discussion and ask a respected member of your group to sit next to you and offer support. If one person's behavior is demanding more than their share of your attention, ask someone to sit with that person and guide them, so that you can keep your attention more on the group as a whole.

Between meetings, do not hesitate to reach out to people outside your group for guidance and perspective. Often, the person with nothing at stake in a situation is in the best position to clearly see the dynamics of the decision-making process.

Whatever kind of help you need and wherever you find it, get it. Do not resign yourself to "going it alone." Asking for help is a sure sign that you understand the importance and complexity of the facilitator's job.

Search Committee Challenges

BY MARCIA J. PATTON

I was once part of a team of twelve people tasked with finding a new leader for a national religious organization. We wanted to do our work faithfully, and we decided at the beginning that we would make our decision by consensus. Our chairperson was very good at her work, but like everyone else in the group, she was deeply invested in the outcome. The group asked the youngest member to serve as chaplain. She did well at leading centering exercises at the beginning of each meeting but seldom offered much beyond these opening moments. Someone from outside the group took minutes but was not given a voice in the meetings. Her role was strictly administrative: to record outcomes, make arrangements for us to meet, and take care of the group's logistical needs. The team hired a search firm to find candidates, and someone from this firm participated in the meetings. This person was not a part of the organization that was choosing a new leader, but he did not remain neutral in the discussions. He had a favorite among the candidates, which gave him a stake in the decision. He didn't fully understand the workings of the organization, so we asked him not to share his opinions about the candidates; he did anyway.

We first narrowed down a long list of people to about ten likely candidates and had initial in-person interviews with them. At the recommendation of the search firm person, we then narrowed the list to four. Then all the search team members traveled to a central location to hold second in-person interviews with the four final candidates and make a decision, all in one day. (This was before pandemic travel restrictions and the increased use of virtual meetings that they have engendered.)

By 10:00 p.m., one of the four people had been totally eliminated by consensus. Eight people were in support of the next candidate. There was also strong support for the other two candidates, but the group focused on the first acceptable candidate, who was the "pick" of the search consultant. Three people had strong reservations about this candidate, and I was completely unable to support his appointment to the position. I had told the group the first time we saw his name that I had strong reservations about him, and in the course of the interviews, my opinion of him did not change.

Because everyone on that team had a stake in the decision, no one was managing the process. As a "hold-out" from agreeing to support the majority's choice, I felt between a rock and a hard place. Many of us had early flights the next morning, and people felt that we had to make a decision that evening. As a participant,

I could not look at the process from a facilitator's point of view. That wasn't my role. Someone said, "We'll just have to report that we can't make a decision." Hearing this panicked me, as this had been the outcome of a previous team's search for someone to fill this position. I joined with the other "dissenters" in agreeing to the choice with strong reservations (four on the scale of levels of consensus; see Chapter 3, Step 7). In a nod to the dissenters, the team agreed to call this person to the position with the provision that he would be told about the four people with strong reservations.

It was a disastrous decision. The reservations I had had about the person we chose proved to be true; he was not able to work effectively within the organization's structure. For example, he tried to circumvent the executive committee when facing major decisions, and he made public statements that alienated significant groups within the organization. He suffered a heart attack about eighteen months into his tenure and was not able to return fully to work. He resigned before any action was taken to dismiss him.

How different this process would have been if there had been a person in the meeting whose only job was to attend to the process and who did not have a stake in the outcome. They could have reminded us that a decision did not have to be made that night. We could have continued to deliberate by conference call another day after we had all returned to our homes. We could have considered the second and third candidates and been able to see if there was stronger agreement on one of those early in the evening before we were exhausted. The experience, and most likely the outcome, would certainly have been different. We re-learned the hard way how important it is to have a facilitator who is neutral and has no personal stake in the outcome.

Notes
1. See https://www.kscopeinstitute.org/free-resources.

CHAPTER FIVE
Consensus Takes Time

The most common reason people give for rejecting consensus as a decision-making process is that it takes too much time. Many people argue that the "press of time" precludes using consensus; even worse, many groups stop using consensus in the middle of addressing an issue by claiming that the group is "out of time" or there is "no time" for more discussion.

In reality, time as a limiting factor is a human construct, and succumbing to this artificial pressure often leads to trouble, especially when it comes to consensus. Most decisions that we consider urgent are not. If the roof of the building has fallen in or people are bleeding, the situation is truly urgent, of course, but too often, we behave as though the roof has fallen in when it really has not.

It is easy to confuse importance with urgency and act as though the more important an issue is, the more quickly a decision must be made. Actually, the opposite is true. Even when an issue seems to meet Steven Covey's Quadrant I criteria of "urgent and important,"[1] it's a good idea to take a moment to consider what might happen if you do not rush the decision. Usually, no true harm would be done, and taking the extra time to thoroughly discuss an issue often leads to a decision that works for everyone and therefore does not have to be revisited. As Coach Wooden said, "If you don't have time to do it right, when will you have time to do it over?"[2]

Some people in your group may want to make a decision quickly for personal reasons, perhaps out of fear of losing control of the situation or because they are more comfortable acting than deliberating. Also, many people are so used to plowing through agenda items as quickly as possible that they can't imagine any other way to take care of business. In these situations, the facilitator and others in your group need to advise caution against hurrying. Unless the group is already in general agreement about an issue, it is virtually impossible to place a strict time limit on discussion and also reach authentic consensus.

It is important to resist outside influences that may pressure your group to meet an external deadline. These pressures can come from any direction. A funding organization may be offering a grant with a deadline for applications. Political or social justice campaigns may seek your endorsement for an action on a specific date. The meeting may have to end at a certain time because people have planes to catch, or the childcare provider is leaving.

When your group feels pressured from outside to meet a deadline, for whatever reason, resist the urge to let an external force push you to make decisions that disregard the views of part of your community. It is better to withdraw from whatever collaboration has opened your group to external pressure than to let the wider world dictate how you do your work. This is another good opportunity to collectively take a moment to honestly assess the impact of waiting to make a decision. Most often, the worst that would happen is that an opportunity might be lost; in other words, there would be no dire consequences.

The truth is that time is often the best resource we have for making good decisions. The "press of time" is often given as a reason to abandon consensus when the way forward seems unclear. However, this is the point when perseverance is most important, to make sure that everyone in the room comes to the point where they can live with the decision. Especially if some participants are asking for more discussion or need more information about the issue, continued deliberation is exactly what you need.

In many cases, the best course of action is to set aside the issue until a future meeting. This time between meetings is not a time for avoiding thinking about the issue or gathering arguments to buttress your point of view. Rather, it is time for all the people involved to think about and informally discuss the issue with others, especially those with divergent views. Respected elders of the community can help initiate these casual conversations and keep them exploratory rather than confrontational. By the time the issue comes up again in a formal meeting, many people may have evolved their thinking about it, and the points on which people were stuck are often ready to be resolved.

Furthermore, when you choose to give an issue all the time it needs for your group to reach consensus about it, you demonstrate that the people in the community are more important than any one action the group might take. Even when an issue seems to be of tremendous importance, honoring the value of the people involved requires you to take however much time is necessary to include everyone in the decision-making process.

Resisting the urge to place time limits on discussion benefits everyone. Marcia is enough of an introvert that she likes to have time to think through her ideas in detail before taking a position on an issue, so she particularly likes the opportunity consensus offers to hear all points of view before having to state her choice. Nora is enough of an extrovert that talking things through with others helps her to work out what she thinks, so she particularly likes the opportunity consensus offers to have in-depth discussions. Both of us agree that pushing the "we're out of time and we must have a decision" attitude is not only a bad form of consensus but also bullying.

There are times when decisions must be made quickly. If the roof has actually fallen in, of course, something must be done immediately. However, a large group can never manage an emergency response effectively. When an emergent problem arises, your group needs to empower a small sub-group or committee to address the situation. Be sure to clearly define the resources and scope of authority you are giving the smaller group and require them to make decisions by consensus. In this way, people in the smaller group know what decisions they can make and when they need to come back to the larger group to report on progress, request more resources, or present long-term issues identified by the emergent situation.

As a consensus-based community, it is much easier to respond effectively to emergent situations if you have already established committees or sub-groups dedicated to specific areas of responsibility. For instance, every Quaker congregation that has a meetinghouse also has a committee dedicated to maintaining the building and grounds, so when something breaks, there is no need to even bring it up in a meeting for business, except as a report.

If your group thinks an issue is too important to entrust to a sub-group, then by definition, it is an issue that deserves to be given all the time necessary for the group to reach authentic consensus. Sometimes an issue seems so pressing that you feel you must make a decision immediately. This is the moment when you need to take a collective breath and honestly assess how emergent the situation is and how important the decision is for your group long-term. In our experience, there are almost no decisions that must be made both immediately and also by the whole community.

Most important for faith communities, when you allow plenty of time for a decision to emerge by true consensus, you also make space for God to participate in your process. When you push a decision through in a hurry, you close off that possibility. When Jesus was on his way to Jairus' house to see his sick daughter, someone touched his robe, and he unexpectedly felt power flow out from him. Against the advice of his disciples, he stopped and took the time to talk to the sick woman who had touched his robe, and she was healed (Mark 5:25-34). If Jesus had hurried on because there was "no time," he would not have made the opening for God to come in and heal the woman. Giving your time to follow a true consensus process is giving up working in "human time" to work in "God's time." To walk humbly with God, as Micah 6:8 states, we must slow down our rush to "get it done."

Buying New Chairs by Consensus
BY NORA J. PERCIVAL

My Quaker meeting has a large, beautiful worship room (sanctuary) with one entire wall of windows looking out on trees and a lake. It is a deeply restorative and inspiring place to worship. It does not have benches or other stationary seating, and we have chairs that we arrange in various configurations for different events (usually in concentric circles for Sunday morning worship). Quakers in unprogrammed worship basically sit still for an hour, which is easier for most people if they sit up quite straight. This means that the best chairs for a Quaker meeting have padded seats and backs and almost a right angle between the two (almost unheard of in standard chair designs).

When I first joined this meeting in 2003, the worship room was filled with molded plastic stacking chairs with aluminum legs, the kind that was popular in the 1960s and is almost impossible to sit up straight in for any length of time. The meeting had been using these chairs for decades by then. However, many of us hated the chairs and had difficulty settling into worship while sitting in them. Some people felt that we should not spend our funds on our own comfort, but eventually enough people wanted new chairs that we began the process of replacing our old ones.

We knew it would be expensive to acquire 250 chairs, and we wanted to make sure that we would like the new chairs well enough to use them happily for many years. Being Quakers, we knew it would take some time to get just what we wanted. In the end, it took almost three years, but we have wonderful chairs that, more than ten years later, everyone still loves. When Quakers from other meetings worship with us, we actually get compliments on how comfortable our chairs are. Here's how we did it:

1. People who wanted new chairs took their request to the Facilities Committee, a standing committee tasked with maintaining the meeting's buildings and property. Facilities asked the meeting for business (made up of all community members who choose to participate) to approve replacing the chairs in the worship room. The meeting did so (by consensus) and created an ad hoc committee to research our options and bring back to the group a specific chair-acquisition proposal. This took about three months.

2. The ad hoc committee met once a month. In the committee, we first reached out to other churches to see if any of them were getting rid of chairs we might be able to use. We bought a set of cast-off chairs for a very low price and sold our molded plastic chairs to a used furniture dealer specializing in that era. This meant that we acquired the chairs virtually for free. However, although the "new" chairs were more comfortable than what we had been using, they were not really comfortable. We had been working on this for more than a year, but we did not want to settle for less than the best we could get, so we kept looking.

3. We found a custom church chair manufacturer and ordered a sample chair in the style we liked. We also ordered samples of several upholstery fabrics that we thought would go well with the carpet and drapes in the worship room.

4. We put up the fabric samples on a wall in the meeting room and asked people to submit their preferences to the committee in writing. The samples and box for comments remained in

the worship room for several months while we tested the chair design.

5. We placed the sample chair in the worship room and asked people to try it and submit their opinion of it to the committee in writing. Many people sat in the chair for a few moments before and after worship, and a different person sat in it for the whole meeting for worship each week. The chair and the box for comments remained in the worship room for more than a month.

6. The back of the chair was too slanted for most people, so we asked the chair manufacturer to make a sample chair with a straighter back. When we received the new sample, we repeated the process of testing the chair over several weeks.

7. The back of the chair was still too slanted for most people, so we asked the chair manufacturer to make a sample chair with an even straighter back. The manufacturer could not believe we were asking for this, and it took several communications back and forth to persuade them to make a third sample for us. We received the new sample and repeated the process of testing the chair over several weeks.

8. The third sample was comfortable for everyone who sat in it. We asked the business meeting to approve the chair design and fabric we proposed, which they did by consensus. Then we placed our order. A couple of months later and almost three years after we started the process, we finally received our perfect new chairs. We kept some of the "interim" chairs for use in other parts of our building and donated the rest to a smaller, struggling group that needed chairs.

My meeting now has wonderful chairs that everyone loves, and the process of acquiring them brought the community closer together. The most notable ingredients of this successful consensus process were the relationship between the whole group and the sub-group and the meeting's attitude toward time.

A small group of people were really interested in getting new chairs; these were the "issue leaders." They brought their concern to the whole group and offered to participate in efforts to address it. The meeting created a small sub-group to do the time-consuming research and development (R&D) work and make preliminary choices. Many of the issue leaders joined this group. As part of doing the R&D work and considering options, the sub-group ensured that everyone who would use the new chairs, the "stakeholders," had plenty of opportunities to voice their opinions and concerns. This arrangement meant that the people with the most interest in the decision did the bulk of the work, yet everyone had a chance to be heard and have their opinions included.

The group also gave the process all the time it needed. We acknowledged at the start that this was not an emergency. We had been sitting on uncomfortable chairs for decades; taking a few months or even years to replace them was acceptable, as long as we got the chairs we wanted in the end. We already had a few "odd" chairs in the worship room that had been brought in for specific individuals who could not sit comfortably in the plastic chairs. They remained in use by these people throughout the long process of acquiring new chairs, relieving pressure on the committee to find new chairs in a hurry. (One clear sign that we got the right chairs is that there are no more "odd" chairs in the room; everyone is comfortable in the new chairs.) Also, we knew we would be a congregation for many years into the future, so it was worth getting it right. We chose to get it right the first time, so we would not have to do it over, and time has shown that we did just that.

Notes

1. Steven Covey, *The 7 Habits of Highly Effective People* (New York: Free Press, 1988).

2. John Wooden, UCLA Bruins men's basketball head coach, 1948–1975.

CHAPTER SIX

Dos & Don'ts

The basic concepts of consensus are not hard to understand. However, doing it well takes practice. Here are some tips for doing consensus well, learned through decades of using it in our faith communities.

1. Practice. As we have said before, it is important to start using consensus for quotidian business so that, when a contentious issue arises, your community already knows how to use the process effectively. Use committee meetings, event planning groups, and other more casual group meetings as settings for learning the process while making decisions that forward the group's work but are not too controversial. Practicing it on everyday decisions makes it easier to use when complex or difficult decisions arise. People already know the process and are more likely to trust it, because they have seen it in action over time. They are likely to have seen how it has worked in their favor, or at least how all voices were heard. If you have enough interest in your group, you can also have a training session or two to address an imaginary community issue using consensus. This gives everyone the freedom to try the process with nothing at stake, making it easier to accept and learn from the inevitable mistakes every group makes at the beginning. (See Appendix 5 for suggested imaginary issues to use in training.)

2. Choose consensus at the start. Choose to use consensus at the start of your decision-making process. It is almost impossible to smoothly transition from voting to consensus in the middle of a process. We have tried it more than once, and the stories are not pretty. Even better, make consensus part of your faith community's culture, rather than just choosing to use it for certain decisions. This completely avoids the challenges of deciding when consensus is warranted and having to switch to consensus mid-process when parliamentary procedure is not meeting your group's needs.

3. Once you have chosen to use consensus, stick with it. It is almost never successful to abandon consensus and revert to voting when your group is having trouble moving toward a decision. Remember that the people in the room are always more important than the decision you are trying to reach. This is essential to successful consensus and must remain your group's highest priority when making decisions. If you abandon consensus and take a vote, you are letting the majority speak for everyone, and some people will inevitably feel left out of the decision. You are also devaluing the work the group has done up to that point, confirming for those who are unsure of the value of consensus that it is a waste of effort since it can be abandoned at any time.

4. Have all stakeholders at the table. Do not begin to discuss an issue until all stakeholders are present and participating. This is a non-negotiable requirement for successfully using consensus to make group decisions. It is better to say that a decision cannot be reached with those present and/or absent than to say that, even though "they" (whoever they may be) are not here, you are going to proceed.

One reason consensus works well for Evergreen is that their quorum at all levels of business (executive committee meetings, board meetings, and annual meetings) does not require a certain number of people to be present but does require that at least one person from each caucus is present. This tells every caucus, "If you are not here, we cannot do our work." That statement in itself empowers every caucus, no matter how small.

If one or a few community members are present but declining to participate, take a step back in the process and address their resistance. Don't try to push your community through the consensus process with some members resisting. They will undermine the process and decrease your chance of success.

5. Embrace the messiness. Consensus can be messy. Work on staying engaged in the process, even when the way forward does not seem clear. Embrace the messiness as much as you can. This makes it easier for your group to try different ways to move forward when you feel you are at an impasse. Sometimes you need to seek a new point of view, synthesize contrasting points of view, or just let the matter "season" for a while and revisit it at another meeting. In Quaker business meetings, the facilitator often asks for a few moments of silence when the way forward becomes unclear. This allows everyone's feelings to settle and is often enough to reconnect people to their sense of common purpose.

Tender perseverance can bring clarity and hope when the process feels chaotic. By contrast, trying to force the group forward when it feels mired often ends up with hurt feelings and a poor decision, or worse yet, abandonment of your commitment to inclusive and just decision-making.

6. Be open and flexible. Cultivate attitudes of flexibility and acceptance; be open to having your mind changed. We know that this can be a huge challenge. Most people do not understand the power inherent in this attitude until they experience it repeatedly. However long it takes, this shift in attitude is worth learning, as it is what truly opens you to what God wants you to do, rather than what you think you want to do.

If your group struggles with this, consider "preaching" on it now and then, but only well in advance of a meeting, not in the middle of one. Remind people that consensus in a faith community is ultimately about inviting God's viewpoint into the discussion. If we are not opened to having our minds changed, God's voice is not available to us.

It has been a foundation of Quaker business process for more than 360 years that all participants aspire to enter into a business meeting open to having their minds changed. This is a big part of the success Quakers have found using consensus. On the other hand, although Baptists firmly believe that more opinions are always better, it has never been suggested that anyone should be ready to change their opinion! Nonetheless, Evergreen's Baptist community has shifted its collective attitude in this direction, enabling it to function quite successfully using consensus.

7. Begin discussion as soon as possible. Begin discussing an issue as soon as you know you will have to make a decision about it, regardless of how far in the future the decision deadline is. The earlier you begin to address a decision, the less "charge" there will be when you get to the point where you have to decide. There is a tendency among congregational leaders to protect their congregations by trying to resolve issues before letting others know it's an issue. This practice works against success when using consensus. A group's facilitators should let participants know about issues as soon as they know about them. Make it clear that the group does not have to decide anything right away, but they might want to begin thinking, praying, and/or asking clarifying questions about the issues. In this way, when you are ready to begin the decision-making process, people have already thought about it and are less afraid to deal with it.

8. Don't hurry the decision. Quakers joke that they are the only people who can make something blander by seasoning it, because sometimes it seems like they "season" an issue, meaning continue considering it without making a decision, until everyone is so bored with it that they care much less about what is decided than they do about moving on to other issues. This may seem counter-intuitive in our culture of instant gratification but believe us when we say that rushing a decision too often leads to saying things that need to be unsaid and making decisions that need to be walked back and made anew later. Take your time. It is in taking the time to carefully seek God's will that you can open to solutions that would never have seemed possible at the start of the discussion.

If your group feels completely stuck on an issue and the discussion becomes circular or repetitive, you might try breaking up into small sub-groups to share personal reflections. One good way to initiate this kind of sharing is to ask each person to complete one or both of the prompts, "I wonder . . ." and/or "I notice . . ." Avoid making these sharing sessions formal; don't take minutes or report back to the larger group. Just share and listen to each other. It's amazing how transformative an exercise like this can be in a group committed to seeking unity and inclusivity.

9. Remind people what consensus is. Until your group has experience using consensus, begin each session with a brief description of how consensus works. Ideally, the first time you use consensus, your group spends a long time discussing in detail how the process works, so that a summary description at subsequent meetings is just a reminder of what most or all the participants already know. At the beginning of each meeting, say aloud or give out a printed copy (or both) of the following statement or its equivalent:

> We reach consensus when all of us are ready to live with the decision we are making. We do not all have to endorse it wholeheartedly, but we must all be ready to agree not to

work or speak against the decision once it is made. Until we come to that point, our tasks are to share our ideas respectfully, listen to each other with open hearts, and find together what God wants us to do.

If your group is comfortable with it, we encourage you to read this at the beginning of every business meeting, not just when you are starting to use consensus. People tend to get a bit casual about using any process they think they understand well, and it never hurts to remind them of the foundational goals of the process.

10. Use tools that ensure appropriate, just, and inclusive communication. Use Mutual Invitation or other communication tools that encourage participation and respect, to ensure that every voice has the opportunity to be heard. Some groups prefer to have people share in the order they are sitting (sometimes called *go around the circle*) or to have the facilitator ask each person to speak in turn. We recommend using Mutual Invitation because it invites every person to speak while offering a gracious way to pass for those who don't want to speak. It also encourages people to pay attention to who has and has not spoken, and to share responsibility for ensuring that everyone gets a chance to speak. When practiced regularly, Mutual Invitation can change the way people think about inclusivity in general, increasing each individual's awareness of how well they are welcoming others to participate, both in group meetings and in less formal interpersonal interactions. Mutual Invitation[1] works like this:

> The facilitator or someone chosen by the facilitator shares first. After that person has spoken, they invite another person to share. After the second person speaks, they invite another to share. This continues until everyone has been invited to speak. If someone is not ready to share yet, they say "I pass for now" and invite someone else to speak. If someone doesn't want to say anything at all, they say "pass"

and invite someone else to speak. As each person speaks, everyone else listens, and when it is their turn to speak, they are encouraged to speak their own thoughts without responding directly to anyone else's words. After everyone has had an opportunity to speak, the last person who speaks invites someone who "passed for now" earlier to speak, and then that person invites someone else who passed, and so on. After everyone who wants to has spoken, the facilitator asks if there are clarifying questions and then opens the discussion for less formal sharing.

11. Take time for group reflection when the way forward seems blocked. Sometimes a discussion gets stuck, with some people insistently repeating their views and seeming unwilling to be open to the ideas of others. When this happens, stop the discussion and ask the group to participate in a reflection exercise such as this:

- Invite everyone to get comfortable, close their eyes if they want to, and/or be ready to make notes.
- Ask everyone to respond inwardly to the following questions. Stress that every participant needs to answer all the questions, not just the ones they initially think apply to them. One at a time, with a minute or two of silence between each question for people to consider their answer, ask:
  1. Am I feeling bullied or intimidated?
     a. If yes, why do I feel this way? Has someone said or done something that is triggering this feeling in me?
     b. Can I unite with any part of what the people voicing opposing views are saying? If so, what? If not, how can I unite with them as partners in our shared work without uniting with their statements?
     c. Are there people voicing views in agreement with mine? What are they saying that gives me hope?
     d. How does my relationship with God sustain me at this moment? How can I share this with others?

2. Am I bullying or intimidating others?
   a. Excluding my feelings as much as possible, why do I think my view is right?
   b. Are there people voicing views in agreement with mine? What are our reasons for promoting this view? Which of these reasons do people with opposing views accept as valid? Which do they reject as invalid?
   c. Who gains and who loses if the group chooses my point of view?
   d. How does my relationship with God sustain me in this moment? How can I share this with others?

- Do not ask anyone to share their answers to these questions with the group. The questions and answers are for self-reflection only and specifically not to be shared aloud to strengthen anyone's point of view in the discussion. Once the exercise is completed, take a break for a few minutes to allow people to stretch and use the facilities. Then go back to the issue under discussion, summarizing the main points that had been under discussion before the break.

12. Enlist the help of people experienced with using consensus. Until everyone in your group is comfortable using consensus, invite someone familiar with your group and with consensus to act as a process mentor. Choose someone who has nothing at stake in the decisions under consideration; they must be able to focus solely on the process. Once your group leaders are comfortable using consensus, one of them can act as a process mentor, but for the first few meetings, we encourage you to use the services of someone from outside the group. Be sure to find someone experienced in using consensus in a faith community, as secular consensus processes are often quite different.

13. Limit the size of your group. If there are twelve people or fewer in your group, you can work through the whole consensus process together. If your group is larger, divide into smaller sub-groups to create safe spaces for all participants to feel able to share their thoughts. Ideally, each sub-group should have twelve people or fewer in it. (See Chapter 3, Step 5 for more about setting up sub-groups.)

a. Have each sub-group reach consensus, then have one person speak for each sub-group in the large group. Give all sub-groups an equal voice in the large group, regardless of the relative sizes of the sub-groups. When larger groups make equal room for smaller ones, everyone can truly feel heard. One of the miracles of Evergreen is how the Euro caucus has accepted this equal status with other caucuses. There are usually more Euro caucus members at a meeting than all the other caucuses put together. This has been true from the beginning of Evergreen. For the first several years, the Asian caucus had only a few members at each meeting, and when the Hispanic caucus was formed, it had just three members. Nonetheless, consensus means that every caucus has an equal voice, whether there are three or thirty people in the caucus, and the Euro caucus has supported this from the beginning.

b. When forming sub-groups, consider the power dynamics in the larger group (e.g., male/female, clergy/laity, color/ethnicity), and create the sub-groups as homogeneously as possible. Don't dilute the minority voices in your group by scattering them. Give each minority a sub-group in which they can find their collective voice and then bring that perspective to the larger discussion.

c. Be honest about identifying affinity groups within your community and use them as the basis for creating sub-groups. For example, Evergreen Baptist Association created caucuses based on ethnicity because those were the association's strongest affinity groups.

14. Make sure everyone can hear everyone else. Unless the group is very small, use a microphone and sound system to ensure that everyone hears everyone else, and that no one interrupts or chimes in unrecognized. Appoint one person to be the "mic runner," to give the microphone to each person in turn to speak. Except when using a structured communication tool such as Mutual Invitation, let the facilitator choose the order in which people are recognized to speak. This is a great way to give slow speakers the space to complete their message without more forward people interrupting them.

15. Take minutes of every meeting. Always take minutes of all decisions, including key reasons for them, and have the minutes approved by the group that made the decisions. Choose one or a few people to be recorders and always have them take the minutes. This gives the group's records consistency over time. Also, have the minutes of past meetings readily available for reference.

If you have trouble getting minutes of previous meetings approved at subsequent meetings, develop a process for writing and approving minutes during each meeting. Pause at the end of each agenda item for the recorder to draft a minute and then read it aloud. Ask the group to approve the minute (by consensus) before moving on to the next item. If the group can't approve the minute as written, discuss what needs to be changed, and then give the recorder time to rewrite the minute and read it aloud again. Repeat this process until everyone agrees on the text of the minute. If it is not possible to write a minute that everyone approves, the issue is not settled and needs more discussion. This may take more time than you want it to, but it is the best way to ascertain that you have actually reached consensus.

16. Make sure minutes include reasons. It is vitally important that minutes include key reasons for all decisions. Be sure to date the minutes. Give each agenda item a number, and record any decisions made and/or tasks assigned for each item. Add a brief summary of the discussion, usually without naming individual speakers or directly quoting anyone. For example, the recorder might write: "After discussing concerns about [*fill in brief descriptions of the specific concerns discussed*], the meeting decided to [*fill in the decision made*]." Refine the format as you become more comfortable using consensus and see the role that minutes play in the process. Ask for feedback from respected members of your congregation. Like so many elements of consensus, taking good minutes takes practice.

17. Accommodate all languages. Regardless of what language a person speaks, they want to be heard, and in many American congregations, not everyone speaks English. This can be a challenge in business meetings, regardless of the process used. If your congregation is in this situation, don't let it deter you from using consensus. There are ways to accommodate everyone's needs. If there is only a single person facing a language barrier, you can hire an interpreter to sit with that person, tell them what others are saying, and speak for them to the group.

If several people in your group speak a different language, hire interpreters for both languages to make sure that everyone's words can be understood. This is called consecutive interpretation, which means that, after each person speaks in their chosen language, an interpreter repeats their statements in the other language. In the US, this most often happens with mixed English/Spanish congregations, but it could be any two languages. Once you choose to do this, let everyone know that you will be doing this and follow through with it. It's demoralizing for people struggling with a language barrier to be promised help and then not receive it. This is not the most common method of interpretation, so make sure your interpreters understand what you want them to do.

If you are using sub-groups, it is completely appropriate to use language as one criterion. Be sure to allow time for consecutive interpretation in the large group sessions, both before and after the sub-groups meet.

This clearly takes time, which is an intrinsic dynamic of consensus. If you really want the people in the room to be more important than the decisions you are discussing, you have to devote the time it takes for everyone to be heard. (See Chapter 5 for more about time and consensus.)

18. Evaluate how consensus is working. Measure the effectiveness of the process as you use it. Review your use of consensus, as an issue for group discussion, on a regular basis and at least once a year. Adapt your process in response to concerns raised in these reviews.

Best Intentions

BY JILL WYNNS

Jill Wynns is retired from a long career in public education at the local, state, and national levels. She is also Nora's sister, and when Nora told her about writing this book, she said, "Oh, consensus, easier said than done!" Curious as to why she had such a negative view of the process, we asked her to share with us (and you) an experience of what happens when consensus is not done well.

In my twenty-four years in elected office, I was a member and president of the San Francisco Board of Education and the California School Boards Association. Even before I was first elected to the school board in 1992, I was interested in the growing movement to expand participation in public policymaking. The early nineties were the heyday of shared and site-based decision-making in public education. The San Francisco Parents' Lobby was part of this movement and a strong voice for parents. We advocated for parents to have more influence over schools, school board elections, and local and state education policies. We testified at hearings and met with elected officials. As its president, I was a strong advocate for changing the parliamentary procedure regimen that was, and remains, deeply embedded in the public policy process.

    We formed a school-community coalition, San Franciscans Unified, to advocate for school funding. The heart of this coalition was a partnership between parents and labor unions. A strong foundation of trust grew in the group because we had a common interest in increasing public education funding. Of course, the school district also shared this interest and was more or less forced to participate, but members of either the parents' group or the union were always in the leadership positions. We talked a lot about how we would decide things, which made it easier to make decisions. We trusted each other, and although we talked about what we would do if we disagreed, we never got around to formalizing a "what if" process because we never needed it. We just talked until we came to agreement.

    At this time, the school restructuring movement was in full swing. Teachers, administrators, and parents were demanding more control over their classrooms, their curricula, and even their budgets. Our superintendent, a friend of parents, teachers, and the unions, was skeptical; he thought it would be impossible for schools to focus on the right things. He used to say, "They'll spend all their time arguing about toilet paper," to illustrate how hard he predicted it would be to focus on the important things. Nonetheless, he supported the efforts for change, with a "let's see what you can do" attitude. So, with the enthusiastic support of the teachers' union, San Francisco Unified developed a restructuring program to be run by someone who worked (uniquely) for both the district and the union.

Then the Parents' Lobby got their president, me, elected to the school board, where I immediately began championing school sites making their own decisions. Securing private funding, the board established the Center for Collaborative Change, which we hoped would change everything about how our district operated and maybe even expand beyond the school system. We joined a national project funded by the Ford Foundation, called Improving Schools through Labor-Management Cooperation. Many of us went twice to the Kennedy School of Government at Harvard to study labor-management cooperation. When our professor told me that, if I came to the program again, it should be as a teacher, I felt like I was good at this. This gave me the confidence to believe that I could really help effect fundamental change in our school district's culture.

We talked confidently about reaching consensus, trusting the "talk until you get to where you need to be" experiences we had had in the coalition. We believed that, if we included a sufficient number of options to reach agreement, we would leave room for everybody to be satisfied enough to agree. We particularly liked the "can you live with it?" option because our past experience with everyone involved gave us faith that we could always get to a place where everyone could live with it. The "I can't live with it" option seemed like something that we could always overcome and would never be exercised anyway.

On a wave of enthusiasm, we urged our labor unions to embrace collaboration. We hired consultants to train us to use an interest-based bargaining (IBB) approach and actually started to bargain with the teachers using a profoundly different way of negotiating. In fact, we tried not to negotiate at all but to reach agreements based on our mutual interests. We felt great about this, and we had great success with the teachers, rewriting the whole teacher contract with many profound changes that have had long-term positive impacts. These included changing the vesting process for lifetime health benefits, which has saved the school district from potential bankruptcy and served as a model for the City and County of San Francisco to do the same.

We became more and more optimistic about shared decision-making as we collaborated successfully with the teachers through two contract cycles over several years. However, when we tried to use this bargaining process with other unions, our collaborative efforts failed. One of the sticking points was that other unions, even though they had been participants in our coalition and had been in our training at Harvard, could or would not bargain from a non-adversarial perspective. They had been to the IBB training but still felt that they had to come to the bargaining table with a position. They brought an initial proposal and gave only lip service to the session that begins the IBB process, where mutual interests are identified. Their attitude was, "Sure, let's talk about our common interests, but this is our proposal, and now you have to respond with your own proposal, according to the rules of bargaining; if our agreements can be about those interests, that's great, but if not, oh well." When we tried to use consensus (as we had agreed to do), they would listen and talk, and then inevitably conclude with, "We can't live with that." Worst of all, they refused to answer the question, "What is it about this that you can't live with?" Of course, without their sincere commitment to IBB and consensus, the whole process was doomed. Even more discouraging, the teacher's union had changed leadership and was no longer interested in collaborating based on common interests.

I have come to realize how deeply voting and the name-of-the-game-is-win attitude are an integral part of the way we make decisions in groups, especially when deciding public policy. I still believe that consensus is not only possible but desirable in public policymaking. I don't work in that arena anymore, but I value the experiences I have had and look forward to a time when finding mutual interests becomes a high priority again, and a kinder, less adversarial world re-emerges.

Notes

1. Rev. Dr. Eric H. F. Law, *The Wolf Shall Dwell with the Lamb: A Spirituality for Leadership in a Multicultural Community* (St. Louis, MO: Chalice Press, 1993), 82–83.

CHAPTER SEVEN

Virtual Meetings

Video conferencing technology has been available for many years, though until 2020 its popularity was limited. The software was generally cumbersome to use, and many people were uncomfortable with the format. However, as we became sequestered during the Covid-19 pandemic, millions of meetings around the world transitioned to virtual formats. Technological challenges aside, virtual meetings have advantages, including allowing people to participate regardless of where they are and saving travel time and costs. As a result, many groups will continue to meet virtually for the foreseeable future, regardless of health safety restrictions.

While there are many advantages to virtual meetings, there are also many challenges, particularly when using consensus. For example, many common sharing techniques, such as using a talking stick or going around the circle to give each person a chance to speak in turn, are impossible. Also, in an in-person meeting, the facilitator can observe body language and notice quiet side conversations and meaningful looks between participants. This helps the facilitator gauge what people are thinking and how they feel about the issue under discussion. Unfortunately, this kind of observation is difficult or impossible in a virtual meeting.

It is certainly still possible to use consensus effectively when you meet virtually, but you will probably need to adapt your in-person process to fit the new format. Here are a few helpful techniques we have learned:

- Publish the meeting information at least a few days before the meeting date and in several places if possible. Be sure to include the instructions for joining the virtual meeting, the agenda, the minutes from the previous meeting, and any other relevant documents. If you are using sub-groups in breakout rooms, publish when in the meeting they will happen and how to join them.
- Start the meeting several minutes before the published start time and encourage newcomers to join early. This gives them time to become comfortable with the technology and gives everyone a chance to get to know each other a little by chatting informally, as you would in a meeting room before an in-person meeting starts.
- Review all the steps in Chapter 3 and be sure not to skip any of them. Your goal is for people to feel, as much as possible, like they are in an in-person meeting. It is particularly important to include opening and closing rituals and to review community norms, noting in particular which ones may have to be modified to fit the virtual format. You may also want to create specific group norms for virtual meetings, such as waving both hands for clapping (the ASL sign).
- Make sure everyone's name label is correct; don't be afraid to ask someone to give their full name or confirm the spelling. Especially when someone is new to the group, this is a primary way that people become familiar with the new person. If people join a video-based meeting by phone, change their phone numbers to names, so everyone knows who they are.
- Think about whether or not to allow participants to use the "chat" function to have private or public side conversations. This can be a great way for people to ask questions or share

relevant resources without interrupting the flow of the group discussion, but it can also be distracting. Private side conversations, in particular, can become hurtful and undermine the sense of community you are trying to foster.

- Use screen sharing to show the agenda and other relevant documents. Think of it as the whiteboard or flipchart you might have in a meeting room. Be mindful about who gets to share their screen and how much of the time screen sharing needs to be used. Try not to use it too much, as when a screen is shared, most faces disappear, again undermining the sense of community.

- Think carefully about how you want to ask for a final decision. Asking for a show of fingers to indicate levels of consensus works fairly well in a virtual environment. In the absence of nonverbal cues, this helps the facilitator get a sense of the meeting. This approach is more effective at achieving authentic consensus than asking for a show of hands in support of a decision because it allows people to express more nuanced positions. Experience has taught us that most decisions engender a wider variety of opinions than just "yes" or "no." However you choose to assess support for a decision, never ask for a show of hands to approve a decision and another show of hands to reject a decision, as this is voting. (See Chapter 4 for more about assessing levels of consensus.)

- Build into the schedule periods of unstructured time, especially at the beginning and end of the meeting and in transitions between the large group and sub-groups. These periods of informal interaction are an intrinsic part of the fabric of group work and give people more time to transition internally from one group dynamic to another. They happen naturally when you meet in person; when you meet virtually, you have to create them consciously.

- When your group first decides to transition to a virtual meeting format, have a few informal sessions with little or no agenda, where you can all play with the technology and just visit with each other. Familiarity with the technology helps to reduce the barriers to creating an authentic sense of community.
- Consider using Mutual Invitation in your online meetings, even if you don't usually use it during in-person meetings. It is a great way to encourage everyone to participate in making sure that everyone else gets a chance to speak, and it is unexpectedly well suited to the virtual meeting format. It ensures that everyone gets a turn to speak when other sharing techniques, such as going around the circle, are impossible. Also, by reassuring people that they will definitely get a turn to share their thoughts, it encourages them to keep their mics muted and refrain from interrupting. If everyone can see everyone else on one computer screen, you can easily use Mutual Invitation with the group as a whole. If the group is too large for everyone to appear on one screen, you may need to send participants to breakout rooms where everyone in the room can see everyone else on one screen. Then each room can report back to the larger group, using Mutual Invitation to have one group invite the next.

Several technical tasks need to be done to keep a virtual meeting running smoothly. Someone needs to pay close attention to who is joining the meeting and how they are labeled. Someone also needs to monitor the chat function, if you have enabled it, to see if someone is asking a question and to make sure no one is writing hurtful words. In addition, someone needs to be watching every person's image to see if they are trying to be recognized to speak. This is especially challenging if there are more participants than can fit on a single screen. Unless the group is very small (about six people or less) and everyone is familiar with the technology, the facilitator can't do all these tasks and also facilitate the content of the meeting. They need help. This is best provided by specific individuals assigned to specific tasks in advance. If that isn't feasible, the facilitator can ask for volunteers when the group gathers. The larger your group is, the more important it is for you to have meeting management tasks assigned in advance and given to people who are familiar with the technology.

At the very least, your facilitator should be supported by a **meeting host**. This person's job is to manage who joins the meeting and how their image is labeled. They can also mute participants who are being disruptive or joining the meeting from environments with distracting noises. In extreme cases, they can expel intractably disruptive participants from the meeting.

Depending on how many items need to be shared on the screen, you might want to have a **screen sharing manager**. If you choose to do this, give that person electronic copies of everything that might need to be shared, and perhaps limit screen-sharing privileges to only that person.

You might also want to have a **chat manager**, someone to monitor side conversations. This person's job is both to limit hurtful words and to alert the facilitator of any issues that arise in the chat stream. If you are holding a meeting where interruptions for miscellaneous issues might be problematic, the facilitator can arrange to receive text messages from the chat manager and then decide whether or not the question or issue merits interrupting the main meeting.

If you have many participants, you may need to have a **screen watcher**. This person's job is to constantly scan the participants' images to see if someone is trying to get a turn to speak. If many people want to speak at once, they can keep track of who has raised their hand first and let the facilitator know the order in which to call on people. The screen watcher can be especially helpful when the facilitator calls for a show of fingers to indicate levels of consensus.

Sub-groups are especially useful in large virtual meetings. Even if your community doesn't generally use them during in-person meetings, consider using them when you meet virtually. If you are not going to break into sub-groups at random, ask the meeting host to assign people to sub-groups. However, you divide up, be sure that each sub-group has a facilitator familiar with the consensus process, and if the group is expected to report back, a recorder. Make sure to leave some unstructured time at the beginning and end of the sub-group sessions for people to interact casually.

Virtual meetings are a mixed blessing, like most things. Still, when the alternative is not to meet or to exclude valued members of the community because of mobility or health safety limitations, they are well worth learning to do well.

Precious, Valuable Breaks

BY REV. DOUGLAS AVILESBERNAL

Rev. Douglas Avilesbernal is the current executive minister of the Evergreen Association of American Baptist Churches. Although Evergreen has held meetings of small groups remotely for a long time, the whole annual meeting of all members was held online for the first time in 2020.

The Evergreen Baptist Association gathers annually for fellowship, mutual support, and business related to our communal ministry. About a month after the gathering, the executive committee, of which I am a member, meets to review the event. We read the evaluations and share our own perceptions of what took place.

In 2020, we had an entirely different annual gathering, as COVID-19 forced us to move our entire conference online. As you might imagine, there were a thousand details to attend to, including recreating events in a completely different format. To the credit of the organizing committee, we were able to transform our whole three-day gathering, with only a few months' notice, into something that we hoped would work well enough as an entirely online conference. One choice that helped us greatly was to hire a company to do the tech side of the conference, so the rest of us could concentrate on the content. This was a key to our success, and I recommend doing it when possible.

Nonetheless, this was our first time producing a virtual conference, and we didn't start working on it until after we were well on our way with planning our usual in-person gathering. In the end, it went off as well as it could have, given the circumstances. There was actually a sense of satisfaction on the organizers' part and also reflected in the reviews we received. The pandemic had thrown us a curve, and our community had been nimble enough to adjust successfully.

The gathering went well, but there seemed to have been something missing that we sensed but couldn't really capture. Then the executive committee met about a month after the event for the annual gathering review. We read and discussed the reviews we had received and shared our own impressions of the gathering. Some of what was missing was already clear. For example, we hadn't had worship services like we usually do at the end of each day. We also had not been able to enjoy regular catching-up times, such as shared meals, as we usually have during an in-person gathering.

However, there was something more, though we couldn't name it. We agreed something was missing and set aside a final discussion of the gathering to a later executive committee meeting. Then, as so often happens, small conversations after the executive committee meeting began to illuminate the sense of something missing, and the pieces of the picture started to emerge. People felt cut off too suddenly; some caucus members felt they hadn't been able to express themselves as they usually do. There was a felt sense of not knowing how the rest of the community was doing. Everything pointed to a reduced sense of connection.

The initial temptation was to blame this on the limitations of video conferencing, but as we continued to talk about it, there was a growing sense that there was something more to it. There was a lingering sense among some people that they had not been heard. Then an offhand comment brought it all together. Someone said, "I didn't even get to chat with anyone on my way to the caucus meeting."

Of course! The platform we used is Zoom, which is very focused on efficiency and fast transitions. Such efficiency is prized and even required in the fast-paced business world, but in our environment, opening space for everyone to know they have the time and space to be heard is most important. It finally made sense; we had lost our transition times. We had allowed ourselves to be ruled by the way Zoom is designed to do transitions, rather than focusing on the importance of deliberate transitions. During the planning, it didn't even occur to us that transition time between sessions is an essential part of consensus.

Looking back now, we see clearly that people need time to transition away from a large gathering where they are mostly listening passively into a more intimate space where they need to be more active listeners. We needed to build in time for people to get settled in their new rooms. We needed to schedule several minutes of unscheduled time at the beginning of every session when people could just say hi across the room or message each other in the chat box. This could give everyone enough time to settle in, engage with the new meeting space, and have the casual conversations people usually have as they enter a meeting room.

As I look back, I can see how we missed this. We were so focused on how taxing video conferencing is and how full our days were. We completely forgot about the breaks built into our in-person gatherings by moving physically from one space to another. We condensed our schedule, meticulously packing as much work into our time together as we could so that we could have shorter days with just one or two long breaks. It would have been better to have had longer days with many brief breaks and at least one long one. This would have served us better because the consensus model requires time for people to move through the mental and emotional transitions required for full engagement in the process. Video conferencing tools are designed for efficiency, but for consensus to work well you need time and space for inner transitions. This is what enables you to listen deeply and respond authentically. We went astray because we were too focused on the zero-sum transactional value of time, when we needed to be focused on the value of building community, without regard for the time required to do so.

Epilogue

Working together on this book has been an incredible experience. We were already friends, which went a long way toward helping us collaborate and use consensus to make the myriad decisions involved in a project like this. However, we come from different faith traditions and didn't really expect to find so much common ground in our thinking about faith-based consensus and inviting God into the process. It was a delightful surprise to discover how close our thoughts are on this subject. Our hope is that people of all faiths will find common ground through implementing our ideas.

We also deepened our understanding of consensus as we researched and wrote. Marcia started out thinking that the Quakers already knew all about the process, and Nora assumed that Evergreen Baptists were experts, since they invented their own consensus process. We discovered, though, that a lot of the ideas we have presented here have not been articulated before in either of our faith communities. Our hope is that this book will serve our communities and yours in deepening their understanding of faith-based consensus.

In our conversations with others as we worked on this book, many people asked if we were going to discuss secular consensus, such as the decision-making processes in some co-housing communities and service organizations. We decided early in the project to mostly limit this book to consensus in faith communities, so we could emphasize the God element we believe is present. However, as Jill's story shows, many of the same principles apply whenever groups make decisions by consensus. Although secular organizations may not be able to seek God's will, they can identify mutual interests to work toward together in seeking the common good. The important thing is to shift the intent of the individuals in the group away from advocating for their individual interests and toward seeking the best solution for the group as a whole. (See Chapter 6 for Jill's story about secular consensus.)

We hope this book will become a manual for people seeking to build consensus in their faith communities, and that it will make the process seem less daunting and more accessible. We hope it gives you the courage to try using consensus. We know that, if you do, it will change your community for the better. We look forward to hearing how you use the ideas we present here and what kind of impact using consensus has on your community. Please send your stories to us at sacred.decisions@yahoo.com.

As you join us in our journey to a more just and inclusive world, may God be with you.

APPENDIX 1

Sample Agenda

1. Opening according to your community tradition.
2. Introductions.
3. Description of the consensus process.
4. Review of the communication tools and/or group norms your community uses.
5. Review of the agenda.
6. Division into sub-groups, if you are using them. Be sure the sub-groups include in their agendas:
   a. Review of the minutes of the previous meeting in preparation for approving them.
   b. All items that will be presented for discussion or decision when the large meeting reconvenes, so that the sub-group can prepare a position to contribute to each item's discussion.
7. Re-formation into a single large group with a brief re-opening comment or reading.
8. Review of the minutes of the previous meeting to remind everyone what has recently been decided. If your group does not approve minutes at the time they are written, approve them at this point.

9. Main agenda item(s), preferably only one or a few. This includes new and ongoing business that needs discussion and/or decisions. If there is a major issue in this part of the agenda, try to hold over other items to a future meeting to ensure that you have plenty of time for the major issue. (Items 9 and 10 are often switched.)

10. Routine agenda items that do not require discussion or decision, such as financial reports, committee reports, and announcements. (Items 9 and 10 are often switched.)

11. Closing.

APPENDIX 2
Sample Communication Tools

Mutual Invitation[1]

The facilitator or someone chosen by the facilitator shares first. After that person has spoken, they invite another person to share. After the second person speaks, they invite another to share. This continues until everyone has been invited to speak. If someone is not ready to share yet, they say "I pass for now" and invite someone else to speak. (They are invited again to share after everyone else has spoken.) If someone doesn't want to say anything at all, they say "pass" and invite someone else to speak. As each person speaks, everyone else listens, and when it is their turn to speak, they are encouraged to speak their own thoughts without responding directly to anyone else's words. After everyone has had an opportunity to speak, the person who speaks last again invites someone who "passed for now" to speak. The person who is invited a second time to speak, after speaking or passing, invites someone else who passed, and so on until everyone has been invited again. After everyone who wants to has spoken, the facilitator asks if there are clarifying questions. Then the Mutual Invitation process is complete, and the meeting moves into less structured discussion.

It is a great tool for getting initial ideas/concerns/reactions on the table. It is also a great tool for checking to see where a small group is on an issue.

Talking Stick

When building consensus, it is important to ensure that people speak one at a time and to allow time for everyone to speak. One effective way to manage this is to use a "talking stick." This doesn't have to be an actual stick; it can be a rock, a candle, a book, or any object that has meaning for the group and can easily be passed from hand to hand. The person who holds the "stick" is the only person allowed to speak. When they are finished, they pass it back to the facilitator or directly to the next person recognized by the facilitator to speak.

It is important when using the talking stick for the facilitator to control who speaks next. If people are allowed to pass the stick to whomever they choose, there is a risk that one faction will dominate the discussion simply by passing the stick back and forth among themselves and not allow others to speak.

Notes

1. Rev. Dr. Eric H. F. Law, *The Wolf Shall Dwell with the Lamb: A Spirituality for Leadership in a Multicultural Community* (St. Louis, MO: Chalice Press, 1993), 82–83.

APPENDIX 3
Sample Group Norms

RESPECT Guidelines

RESPECT Guidelines[1] are a set of group norms presented as a mnemonic.

R reminds people to take *responsibility* for what they say and feel without blaming others. You are encouraged to use "I" statements and to reflect your opinion without blaming others.

E reminds people to use *empathetic* listening. You are encouraged to listen without judgment, to listen with your whole self.

S reminds people to be *sensitive* to differences in communication styles. Some people talk directly, others spiral to their point, and others take a different path. No path is correct; make adjustments for the paths that others take.

P encourages people to *ponder* what they hear and feel before they speak. The old adage, "think before you speak," is another way of saying this. Ask yourself why you need to speak at this moment.

E encourages people to *examine* their own assumptions and perceptions. You may be ready to say something like "everyone knows," but before you do that, check that assumption; is that really true? Checking your assumptions and perceptions might lead you to a different insight than you thought you had.

C reminds people to share **constructively** for the community's benefit and to maintain a safe space for everyone. Check that what you want to share is helpful to the community and therefore worth sharing. If it will hurt someone, don't share it.

T encourages people to **trust** the process. It is easy to become frustrated when it seems like it's taking forever to come to a decision or when one person or faction is stubbornly attached to their point of view. When the frustration builds, trust that consensus really can bring your whole group, together, to a decision that everyone can support. The more you use consensus correctly, giving each step the time and attention it needs, the easier it will be to trust the process.

Good Order of Friends (GOOF)

Gather to address community concerns as a community.

Open to the Spirit working through the people as a group, including opening to the possibility of having one's mind changed during the discussion.

Observe how the sense of the meeting evolves as people share their thoughts.

Have *Faith* that God is working through you and will lead your group to the best decision for your community.

Notes

1. Rev. Dr. Eric H. F. Law, *Inclusion: Making Room for Grace* (St. Louis, MO: Chalice Press, 2000), 64, https://www.kscopeinstitute.org/free-resources.

APPENDIX 4

Levels of Consensus

1. Have whole-hearted support for the decision.
2. Have slight reservations about the decision but will support it.
3. Have some reservations about the decision but will support it.
4. Have serious reservations about the decision but will support it.
5. Have major problems with the decision and will not support it.
6. Have one or more questions or concerns about the decision that, if addressed, may allow them to support it.

APPENDIX 5

Suggested Issues to Use for Practice

1. **The situation:** The church has agreed that the building needs to be painted. They have the money available to paint it. Everything is decided but what the color should be.

2. **The situation:** The church has been asked to host a homeless shelter. The church has usable space available.

3. **The situation:** A congregation from another denomination and ethnic group has asked the church if they can meet in the building. Most of its people do not speak English as their first language, if at all. The church is not used late on Sunday afternoons when they would like to meet.

4. **The situation:** The youth of the church have asked to have exclusive use of a room in the church that no one is currently using. They want permission to decorate it as they choose and hold their weekly meetings there.